Teaching

Success

The BRAIN-*friendly* Revolution in Action!

Mark Fletcher

Ponder Point...

I believe, unless there are increased efforts to develop an approach to education which balances the rational with the intuitive .... truly sustainable development is doomed.
(H.R.H The Prince of Wales – BBC Reith Lecture May 2000)

Foreword by Sir Christopher Ball

As a learner, I believe I can learn anything – provided the conditions are right! As a teacher, I believe I can teach anybody anything – with the same proviso ... Learning is a natural instinct, and teaching an art that can be mastered. This book is all about the conditions for successful teaching and learning. Read it, if you want to know what they are.

I like to learn in a '7C' environment. The seven Cs are: choice, challenge, clarity, confidence, comfort – and two more I haven't so far identified. **Teaching for Success** provides plenty of ideas for the missing concepts. But I have no doubt about the first five. Learners thrive when they can choose what and how they learn. They like a challenge, but hate threats. They require clarity – a precise description of what constitutes successful learning in any particular case. Confidence and self-esteem are necessary conditions for learning. They are so important that for most people they are by themselves sufficient conditions for success. Call me soft, but I like to learn best when I am comfortable.

Are you sitting comfortably? Then I'll begin . . . Turn to page 19 (or any other page) and enjoy this remarkable book. Mark Fletcher, the author, was one of my student undergraduates many years ago. I wish I had been able to read **Teaching for Success** at the beginning rather than the end of my career. I expect he does too. But it's never too late to learn!

Sir Christopher Ball is Co-Chairman (with Professor Susan Greenfield) of the 'Learning of the Brain' Royal Institution seminars 2000, Chancellor of the University of Derby, and Patron of the Campaign for Learning. He was formerly Director of Education at the Royal Society of Arts, and Chairman of the National Institute for Careers Education and Counselling.

Brain-friendly is a Registered Trademark of English Experience™

Published by
English Experience 2000
Reprinted 2001

©Mark Fletcher and Richard Munns
Illustrations by Mark Fletcher
Edited by Richard Munns
Cover Design - Phil Chandler

ISBN 1 898295 62 X

Printed in Great Britain by Hythe Printers Ltd, Hythe, Kent

English Experience
25 Julian Road, Folkestone, Kent CT19 5HW, England
Telephone/Fax: (44) 1303 226702
Email: englishexperience@dial.pipex.com

Teaching for Success

The BRAIN-*friendly* Revolution in Action!

Mark Fletcher

What this book is about

AT LAST it's happening!

We are witnessing a learning revolution which though it will make use of the astonishing potential afforded by Information Technology, will itself be more profound, coming as it does from new understandings of our development as individuals and within our communities. We are talking about huge leaps in knowledge at the interface between neurological research and the application of that information to best practice in the classroom.

Getting the most from this book . . .

Teaching for Success is written to be **a good read for teachers (and parents, students, lecturers, educationalists, and anyone interested in learning)**.

As such, like a lesson, it should be informative, participatory, stimulating, challenging, fun - and have a positive pay-off. The question for each lesson is *"What can the students do when they go out of the classroom door that they couldn't do when they came in through it?"* Judge this book by the same practical standards.

I trust that at the very least it will reaffirm beliefs you hold about the values of teaching (and that is no small thing).

I confidently expect it *to open some doors, start some chains of thought, provide some tools, ring some bells* which you will develop to make your personal relationship with teaching even more fulfilling.

You will need...

★ to flick through it and see what catches your eye

★ to feel free to write on it, colour it, personalise it

★ to compare its observations and claims with your own experience

★ to give it a fair chance before you make judgments

★ to take seriously the things which strike you as important

★ to put it down now and then and have a good stretch!

   ...but before doing any of that

─────────────────────────────────────── *Challenge*

Please jot down three "big questions" you have about learning and teaching. Is there a matching of interests with those opposite?

   ★

   ★

   ★

★ Can we be better teachers/learners by getting more of the brain involved? If so, how do we do it?

★ How does memory work? What skills should be available to help our students remember things?

★ Is there (neurologically) such a thing as intelligence (or intelligences) or are we really talking about 'talent', 'gifts', 'aptitude'?

★ Are there such things as 'critical learning periods', 'differences between male and female brains', 'alpha learning' states? If there are, what response should we make?

★ Are different 'learning styles' a neurological reality? If they are, do we acquire them or are they in-built? How can busy teachers differentiate between and teach to different styles?

★ What, in brain terms, is 'intuition'? What is 'creativity'? What is 'imagination'? How do we protect, value and develop them?

★ How can we create an optimum 'external' and 'internal' environment for learning?

★ What is the role of 'music', of 'self-esteem', of 'stress' in learning?

★ Do holistic approaches work for subjects such as maths or science – and how do they relate to exams?

★ How can we help the significant number of students who are 'truanting inwardly' or otherwise not getting much from their education?

★ How do I, the teacher, protect my 'self' - and also develop as a person through what I'm doing?

★ What could a Brain-friendly education system look like?

Teaching for Success will provide answers to some of these questions, tentative pointers on others, and a 'don't know yet' to others.

It is a resource and, therefore, will be used differently by different people. I think it will excite – but also cause some frustration at what we don't know. The action from that excitement and frustration will move us on so that, in twenty years' time, we will look back and see how the landscape of the dinosaur age, in terms of understanding learning, is being reshaped by the **Brain-friendly revolution!**

CONTENTS
sequenced as a list

CONTENTS
presented as a mind map

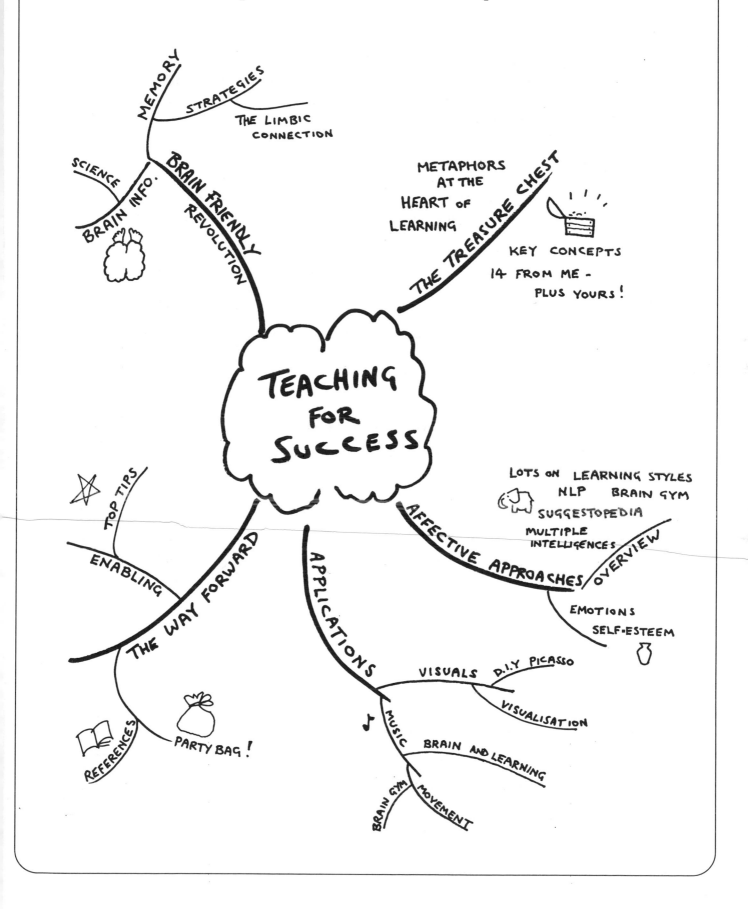

Challenges and Ponder Points

Teaching for Success is a book to dip into. The sections stand on their own, but you will not read very far without coming across a **Ponder Point**. These are quotes gathered from a wide range of sources - ancient philosophers, newspaper columns, poets, public figures, and that well known educationalist, *anon*.

Please read each one several times before moving on because they contain relevant and thought-provoking insights. The **Challenges** ask you to test what you are reading against your own experience and assess if it makes a difference to your situation. Let's make a start with a quote that has been pinned on my cloakroom wall for over a decade! In that time dozens and dozens of visitors have asked if they can have a copy.

Ponder Point...

Until one is committed, there is hesitancy,

the chance to draw back, always ineffectiveness.

Concerning all acts of inititative (and creation)

there is one elementary truth, the ignorance of which

kills countless ideas and spendid plans –

that the moment one commits oneself,

then providence moves too.

All sorts of things occur to help one

that would never otherwise have occurred.

Goethe

Challenge

To gather impressions quickly, flick through the book now and jot down the topic which you think will interest you most.

Your Amazing Brain

This book highlights the importance of brain research in eventually providing a scientific basis for pedagogy. This understanding of what the brain is, and of how we learn, will provide teachers with a rationale for some of the things which we feel intuitively 'work' in the classroom. It will also explain in brain terms, why some things 'go wrong', and provide a sound basis on which to justify new approaches.

I will frequently be referring to aspects of brain functioning in relation to teaching. The following pages provide an overview of what every teacher should know about the greyish, crinkled-on-the-surface, walnut-shaped, porridge-textured, 1.3 kilo marvellous lump between our ears!

porridge!?

NOTE This information is presented by a teacher for teachers. Anything said here about the brain is likely to be a gross simplification, but should at least be a useful guide. Those wishing to go further into neuro-science can find references in the book list to enable them to do that.

Findings from research into how the brain 'works' are rapidly moving into the public domain. As a result, changes are taking place in how we view learning and teaching, and in our expectation of what is possible. Teachers can now apply these insights to practical classroom situations.

Do you recall any journal article, or TV or radio programme, which said something important to you on this subject recently? For me, awareness of this popularisation began a few years ago with the Sunday Times 'Brainplan' series, the 1994 BBC lectures 'Journey to the Centres of the Brain' given by Professor Susan Greenfield (Oxford University) and Paul Robertson's 'Music and the Mind' TV series.

At the beginning of this new Millennium we had 'Brain awareness' week, with a big focus on 'what happens between the ears'.

The interface between education and neuro-science is no longer an area of esoteric speculation for specialists. It is of up-front importance for students, parents, and especially, because we are at the cutting edge of implementing best practice, for teachers. From the platform of new knowledge (or in many cases, from a new and viable rationale for things we already had a hunch about) we educators can launch the 'Brain-friendly Revolution'. If this sounds remote to you as you prepare tomorrow's lesson for unmotivated teenagers, or grab a quick coffee to get through the next hour's adult education, stay with me !

This revolution will come about because of widespread discussion of standards; because of the industry-led demand for frequent and rapid retraining at the workplace; because of the pressures of increased leisure opportunities for improved life-long learning; and because we are beginning to see what is involved and how **we** can make it happen!

Successful learning depends to a large extent on

- How people feel about what they are doing (motivation, self-confidence)
- The opportunities they have (quality of teaching, resources, and help in becoming autonomous learners)
- Having the right *attitude* to learning, *skills* to be able to learn, and *access to the knowledge*

WHAT EVERY TEACHER SHOULD KNOW
It's a 'one-off'

Firstly, we should know that every brain (even those of identical twins) is unique, and constantly changes as we interpret and re-assess experience. That is to say that no-one else in the world has a brain like yours, and that yours is not the same as it was when you picked up this book. The complexity is amazing. The brain is made up of anatomically distinct regions, and we shall think about the role of each, particularly in relation to teaching and learning. Whilst these different regions appear distinct, they are not autonomous mini-brains but form an integrated system in which the whole is, in some not yet clearly understood way, much greater than the sum of its parts.

This suggests that if we teachers plan lessons which simultaneously engage and stimulate several of these brain areas, our students will become more effective learners because this is how the brain itself naturally operates. Much of this book deals with teaching approaches to achieve that goal. Some of the brain areas do have particular jobs, but we mustn't underestimate how many brain regions are usually involved in any specific function (at least thirty areas of the outer surface of the brain are involved in processing vision, for example). In a similar way each brain area will contribute to many different functions. More is also becoming known about the **plasticity** of the brain, that is, the ability of one area, especially in children, to adapt to experience and take over functions from other, usually damaged, areas.

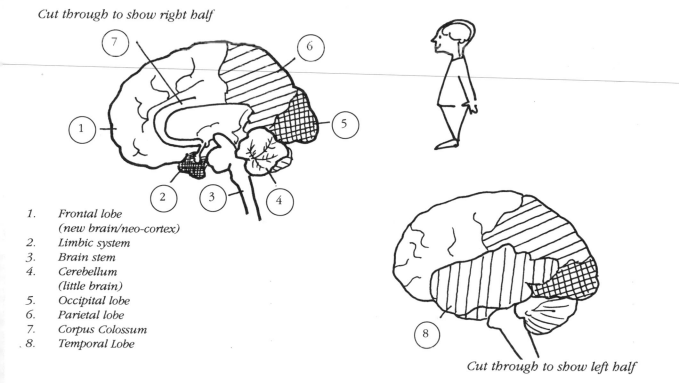

Cut through to show right half

1. Frontal lobe
   (new brain/neo-cortex)
2. Limbic system
3. Brain stem
4. Cerebellum
   (little brain)
5. Occipital lobe
6. Parietal lobe
7. Corpus Colossum
8. Temporal Lobe

Cut through to show left half

Taking a look

Looked at from above, the surface of the brain, the cortex, is seen as two distinct, very wrinkled, hemispheres joined down the middle.....

TWO HEMISPHERES

Much is heard about 'left or right' brain learning, but, if the brain is a complex integrated system, do the left and right hemispheres really have different functions?

The constant interaction of the two hemispheres of the cerebral cortex means that, for most of the time they are effectively one. Nevertheless, brain imaging studies do confirm that, in normal circumstances, each hemisphere has specific strengths. The left hemisphere does seem to favour analytical, logical, time-sensitive processing. The right does seem to be more holistic, intuitive, involved with sensory perception rather than with abstract cognition. Whilst this is a useful distinction for us as teachers, we need to be a little wary of generalisations. Even language, usually regarded as a definite left hemisphere attribute, is organised atypically in about five per cent of people. Again, as teachers, we will be interested not just in the different strengths of the two hemispheres, but in how they engage together in the learning process. Later in the book we will consider why this interaction is so important and how we can facilitate it by using music, visuals and visualisation.

THE CROSS-OVER PRINCIPLE

The Corpus Colossum is a thick band of white tissue (nerve fibres) lying below and connecting the two hemispheres. It acts as a bridge between them. Most sensory input to the brain swiftly crosses via the Corpus Colossum from the incoming side to the opposite side for processing. This applies to visual, touch and auditory input. Smells are the exception to the 'cross-over rule' as they are processed on the same side of the brain as the nostril that senses them. The Corpus Colossum is, on average, thicker in the female brain than the male. Because there are therefore more pathways bridging the two hemispheres, such a difference might facilitate the synthesis of, for example, intuition (right hemisphere) and speech (left hemisphere). These are very early days for making generalisations, still less for drawing conclusions on that issue, but as teachers we need to be aware that research into the brain is beginning to provide help in differentiating how best to present information for learners of different ages, sexes and abilities.

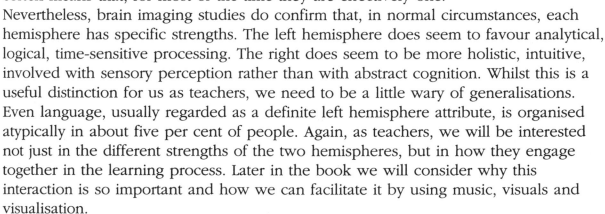

The cross-over principle

Other parts of the brain

THE BRAIN STEM

This is formed from the nerve cells running from the body via the spinal column. It is the most ancient part of the brain in evolutionary terms and is sometimes called the Reptilian, or Reflex brain. Various clumps of cells in the brain stem determine the brain's general level of alertness, and regulate heartbeat, blood pressure, and breathing. Although the brain is roughly two per cent of body weight, about a quarter of heart activity is used to keep it supplied with the oxygen it needs to function effectively. The reflex brain therefore plays a major role in maintaining concentration. We have all probably experienced trying to teach a group of lethargic, oxygen-starved students who have been sitting slumped over their desks (which causes very shallow breathing) for half an hour or more. You can feel the energy level, and the interest, draining away. Movement built into the lesson, some fresh air, the opportunity for the reflex brain to raise the heart beat and get oxygen to where it is needed, will relieve the stiffness and tension caused by sitting still, and greatly improve concentration levels; see page 121 for more on this.

THE CEREBELLUM

This 'little brain' is also connected with movement. Looking rather like a small cauliflower, it perches at the back of the brain stem just below the main brain (the Cerebrum). It forms a smaller proportion of the whole brain in human beings than in creatures such as fish which depend on a constant coordination of feedback from the senses as they swim. Nonetheless, our brains too are somehow connected in a very basic way to the concept of movement. As we move around there is an interaction with an environment that is constantly changing. The Cerebellum has been called the 'auto-pilot' of the brain. The sensory motor coordination it generates underpins skilled movements that can be learned and practised and which become almost subconscious, like catching a ball, dancing, or driving a car. Most of the movements we make are effected by signals sent from the brain stem down the spinal chord and causing the appropriate contraction of muscles. Interestingly, the fine motor movements, the dexterity of our hands in drawing, or playing the piano, or tool making, originate in a different part of the brain, a strip-like band fitting across the top of the highly developed brain and known as the motor cortex. We will meet this fascinating and apparently very basic connection between moving and learning again when we consider learning styles, and bodily - kinaesthetic - intelligence.

Ponder Point...

The human brain is an enchanted loom where millions of flashing shuttles weave a dissolving pattern, always a meaningful pattern, though never an abiding one, a shifting harmony of sub-patterns. It is as if the Milky Way entered upon some cosmic dance.
(Sir Charles Sherrington, 'the grandfather of neuro-physiology')

THE LIMBIC SYSTEM

The area nestling below the Corpus Colossum is generally called the limbic system and for teachers and learners this brain area holds the key to much of our success. Emotions are generated in this region, along with most of our survival appetites and urges. The limbic system comprises a number of closely connected elements. The thalamus is a sort of relay station which directs incoming information to different brain areas for processing. The hypothalamus, together with the pituitary gland, adjusts the body to keep it optimally adapted to the environment. The hippocampus (so called because some say it looks like a seahorse, but for others looks more like a pair of ram's horns) is strongly associated with long term memory and the provision of a context for previous events. The amygdala, in front of the hippocampus, is a store house for emotional memory. It is where fear is registered and, as we shall see later, can under conditions of threat 'high-jack' normal rational behaviour with alarming classroom results. Anxiety is a great inhibitor of memory, and fear of making mistakes or of ridicule, can trigger a 'fight or flight' reaction leading to either disruptive behaviour or opting out. At a basic level, students need the security of 'knowing where they are going' and the surety that if they miss something it will be recycled later on. They need the opportunity to be 'self-investing', that is, contributing something which is felt as being valuable, and also to be operating in a class environment where group support enables mistakes to be seen as steps on a learning ladder and not as demonstrations of stupidity. The role of the limbic system will be very evident when we look at the impact of emotion on memory, and think about self-esteem and confidence.

THE NEO-CORTEX

Cortex is from the Latin for 'bark' as this layer covers the brain as bark covers a tree. It has evolved to be much more extensive in human beings than in any other creature, and as noted earlier, has a convoluted, scrunched-up appearance because a lot is packed into a small space, our skulls. The main wrinkles, valleys and ridges are common to all human brains but the surface detail of each is slightly different. Both the **right and left hemispheres** are visibly divided by major folds into four lobes. The various lobes can, to varying extents, be associated with different functions, (always remembering that the whole brain is an integrated system). At the very back the **occipital lobes** are mainly concerned with visual processing. The top section, the **parietal lobes**, are associated with recognising objects through the senses and the coordination of input from the senses with movement. The parietal cortex is involved in our processes of making associations and is therefore a key region in the forming and storing of memories and in the mysterious process of thinking. To the side, from around the ears to the temples, lie the **temporal lobes** which deal with sound, speech comprehension (usually left hemisphere only) and some aspects of memory. The pre frontal lobes (Neo-cortex, new brain) jut out forward. Neuro-scientists are agreed that the **pre-frontal** cortex is involved in the most sophisticated and integrated brain functions: that of thinking, planning, conceptualising, and the conscious appreciation of emotion. This area also seems to be important for 'working memory' – the framework or context we employ when doing any task, and to have a crucial role in choosing appropriate social behaviour. It is the most significant brain area active in the formation of each individual personality. Finding out more about how such complex and abstract processes occur remains a huge challenge for researchers. As teachers we will want to consider what opportunities for challenge we provide for our students so that this extraordinary and powerful brain resource is brought into action in the learning situation.

One point to make now is that, as we each have a unique brain, it is not surprising that we do not all learn in the same way. The way our own brain learns best is our **learning style**. As teachers we have all met students with strong preferences.

The Visual learners, 'Write it on the board, please. I need to see it before I can understand it'. The Auditory learners, 'Shhh. I need to hear that again.' They are quite happy to listen to a lecture, unlike the Kinaesthetic learners who get frustrated unless they can be physically involved in making, doing, moving.
There is more on learning styles and memory on page 38.

BRAIN CELLS

The brain is composed of two types of cells. The Glia cells (named from the Greek for 'glue') which do the basic biochemical chores, and the **neurons**. It is the neurons which primarily concern us. There are an estimated 100 billion neurons. They are the most important cells in the brain (and the most specialised in our whole body). They form the connecting link between the world we perceive and the world we act on. They carry the complex stream of information from the sense organs and nerves throughout the body to the brain structures, as well as outwards to muscles and organs.

1.	Cell body
2.	Dendrites
3.	Axons
4.	Synapse

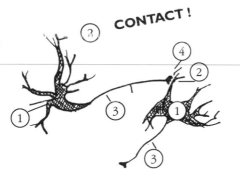

CONTACT!

Memories are made of this!
An electrical impulse is being sent from a neuron (nerve cell) to another across the synapse by chemical neuro-transmitter released by the axon. Millions of these transactions have taken place in your brain as you have tried to make sense of this rather inadequate sketch!

Each of these neurons has a potential for about 60,000 connections with other brain cells!!! The neurons are concentrated in the grey matter, a 2-millimetre-thick layer on the outer surface of the cerebral cortex. This layer appears crinkly because it is scrunched up to pack a large surface into a small area (unfolded and spread out it would be about four times the size of this page). As an idea of the activity going on, imagine an enormous termites' nest …. it seems static, but below the surface is a seething bustle of unceasing movement, a vast confusion of individual insects converging, diverging, overlapping in traffic flows which to the observer appear uncoordinated, and yet obviously form patterns which have meaning and purpose in sustaining the colony.

The brain is an electrical and chemical system. This is not in any way meant to reduce the wonder of spiritual experience, of imagination and creative genius, of powerful and noble emotion, or to suggest that we can account for these things by what we know, or will ever know, about the nuts and bolts of brain cells. The purpose of this explanation is to provide teachers with enough information to understand why, in brain terms, certain attitudes and activities are likely to produce a positive learning environment whilst others have a negative effect.

Each neuron has a cell body. There are a number of characteristic shapes. From the cell body sprout tiny branches called **dendrites**, after the Greek for 'tree'. Most neurons also have a single long fibre stretching from the cell body called an **axon**. Neurons generate electricity. The dendrites act as receivers bringing electrical signals from other cells to their cell body. If these signals are sufficiently strong , their cell body will generate a new signal in response, and the axon will pass this new signal on towards the next target neuron. The scientifically minded may want to know how a neuron generates electricity, or how an individual cell body copes with the barrage of incoming signals and 'decides' what action to take. Please consult one of the excellent neuro-science books in the Reference List for that degree of detail. For most of us it is sufficient to know that next comes a very important chemical step in the process. Neurons are not joined together in a kind of net. There is a gap, a **synapse**, between them. The most common form of cell-to-cell contact is when the tip of an axon forms a synapse with a dendrite. Now the electrical signal has to jump the gap – but how? As soon as the electric impulse reaches the tip of the axon it creates the right conditions to release one of many diverse chemical transmitters into the synapse. The stronger the electrical excitement, the more chemical will be released. The chemical transmitter crosses the gap and 'docks', but only with the specific receptor on the target cell which is precisely made to receive it. The versatility of this chemical system is almost incomprehensible. There are some hundred billion neurons in our brain. Each can make thousands of these synaptical connections. By having different amounts of different chemicals with different actions operating to different extents at different times the brain is in a state of constant chemical change.

Trying to distinguish some very closely connected concepts

Brain – a physical part of the body. Because it is involved in everything we do – and is constantly changing – it is often personalised and given characteristics. These characteristics are more accurately a feature of the **mind**, which is how the brain interprets the brain's interaction with the world. **Consciousness** is to do with a personal awareness of feelings about those experiences ...

Am I being nice to my brain, or is my brain being nice to me?

How do we get all this brain information?

CAT (computerised axial tomography) scans have been routinely used since the 1980s. Brain X-rays are taken in a series of sections as an X-ray tube moves along the axis of the body. The X-rays strike a sensitive scanner connected to a computer. The resulting picture shows the anatomical details of the brain and is particularly useful in identifying abnormalities such as tumours.

EEG (Electroencephalography) uses a number of electrodes placed on the skull to measure brainwaves. Brainwaves are electrical patterns created by rhythmic oscillations of neurons and vary according to the type of brain activity.

PET (positron emission tomography) uses a system of injecting radioactively 'labelled' glucose or oxygen into the blood stream. Oxygen and glucose are two major brain 'fuels'. The more fuel a particular brain area is demanding, the harder it is working. High-energy gamma rays can measure the amount of these fuels being accumulated and differentiate quite subtle regions of brain activity -the difference, for example, between saying words and reading words.

fMRI (functional magnetic resonance imaging) also measures the changes in blood oxygen level in more active brain areas but does so by using radio waves to monitor the magnetic properties of the protein haemoglobin which carries the oxygen. fMRI can give very sensitive readings of an area as small as 1 or 2 millimetres and measure events taking place over just a few seconds.

MEG (magneto encephalography) measures the magnetic field generated by differential electrical activity in the brain and will eventually chart occurring changes very much faster than other methods.

After all that heavy stuff –
A Brain joke

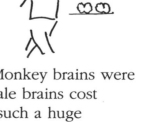

A customer walked into a second hand brain shop to buy a replacement brain, and was surprised to see the brains catalogued in three different price ranges. Monkey brains were priced a £10, female brains cost £20, but male brains cost £1000! The customer asked why there was such a huge difference in price between male and female brains and the assistant replied....(see page 133 for punch line)

A BRAIN-*friendly* checklist
for lesson planning

The technique applies equally to exam preparation lessons, management training, or teaching young learners.

Check 1 for **Left hemisphere**. Will the students recognise a logical progression in this lesson? Does it have a clear timetable fit - or if not, can I explain why it is useful? Are there opportunities for questions and answers, getting to grips with rules, structured practice? Have I got the timing right?

Check 2 for **Right hemisphere**. What is there in this lesson to engage the intuitive, holistic, fanciful faculties? Is there an opportunity for students to visualise situations, to see the 'big picture' not just a small item of target information. Are we using colour for underlining, highlighting? If we are doing skills work, such as summarising or giving talks, are we using non-linear note taking (mind maps)? Have I included music to establish moods (high energy/calming) and to work in conjunction with language (a quiet music 'passive' review of lesson content, or a suggestopedic 'concert reading' session).

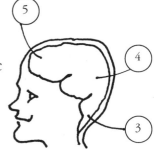

Check 3 for the **Reflex brain**. Where are the occasions for breaking the 'hunched over desk' posture, raising heartbeat and getting good supplies of oxygen pumped around the brain? Have I thought about stretch breaks or times when students are moving around, changing places, collecting material etc.?

Check 4 for the **limbic system**. Memory and emotion are closely associated, so what does this lesson provide so that students 'self invest', contribute their own ideas and feelings, or get positive feedback from colleagues and teacher? Is there an opportunity for team-building, pair and group work? Are the expectations I give about the target material encouraging (eg NOT I'm sorry we've got to do this because it's difficult and not much use but it's part of the syllabus)? *Are my correction techniques conducive to building a healthy 'inner learning environment' showing respect for the learners and avoiding sarcasm or causing embarrassment?*

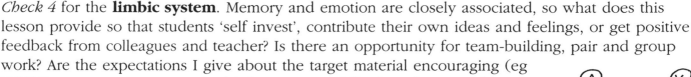

Check 5 for the **neo-cortex (new brain)**. The brain likes to say *'Thank you for that input - now I want to 'claim' the new knowledge for myself.'* Does the lesson contain opportunities for students to be original with the target concepts through role play, tasks etc? Is there a chance for students to experiment and find out how the rules/boundaries operate?

Check 6 for **learning styles**. Can I look at this lesson and say *'Yes. There is a built in safety-net so that auditory, visual and kinaesthetic learners will all be able to get hold of the content'*?

Do you know any learners who display a lot of these characteristics?

* Appears to daydream.
* Talks in phrases or leaves words out when talking.
* Uses fingers to count.
* Draws pictures on the corners of his paper.
* Has difficulty following directions.
* Makes faces or uses other forms of non-verbal communication.
* Displays problems with fine-motor tasks or very structured tasks.
* Can recall places and events but has difficulty with symbolistic representations such as names, letters and numbers.
* May have difficulty in phonics or decoding skills.
* Is on the move most of the time and likes to work standing up.
* May exaggerate when retelling an event.
* Often has a messy desk.
* Has difficulty in completing work on time.
* Likes to take things apart and put them back together again.
* Displays impulsive behaviour.
* Tries to change the world to meet his own needs.
* Likes to touch, trip and poke when relating to other children.
* Gets lost coming to the classroom or forgets what he set off to do.
* May be very good at athletics, but poor in subjects such as language.
* Will give the right answer to a question, but will be unable to tell you where it came from.
* Will often give responses that are unrelated to what is being discussed.
* May be a leader in the class.

Messy? Me? - I'm just naturally creative!

People who themselves are dyslexic, or who teach dyslexic students have commented that they recognise many of these tendencies which are regarded as 'right-hemispheric'. Reading demands that the tiny features of a series of small symbols have to be identified in a fraction of a second, and translated into the sounds that the symbols represent before the meaning of the word can be recognised. The work of Professor John Stein, Professor of Physiology, Oxford University Medical School shows that any impairment in the nerve cells monitoring sound changes, or to the motion of images across the retina such as happens when the eyes scan across print, will affect sensitivity to orthography, the order of letters in a word. A teaching approach which gives plenty of scope for kinaesthetic learning may be very supportive for such learners.

Ponder Point...

In brain terms 2 + 2 = *a lot more than 4!*
If our students are using these different aspects of their brain power, their learning will be a more fruitful experience.
Of course the picture is much more complex (and fascinating) than I have sketched here, but the above does work as a 'rule of thumb' check.

Mind map Review

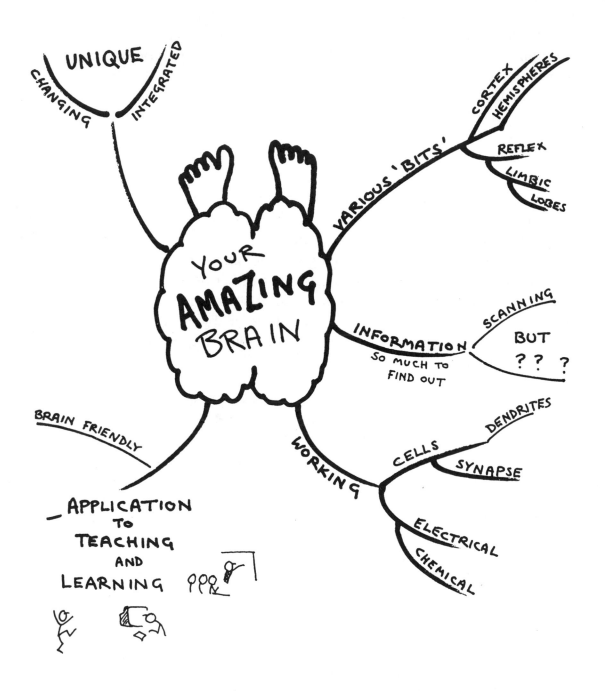

METAPHORS AT THE HEART OF LEARNING

Every teacher has his or her own Treasure Chest. Each Treasure Chest is different – but precious. It contains symbolic reminders of why our job is so important, of what we bring to it in terms of knowledge, skill, personality and who we are. It contains symbols of vital lessons we have learned along the way and gentle reminders of things we mustn't forget.

As I say, each Treasure Chest is very personal, but each is inspirational (especially when the job seems tough and unrewarding) as to what, deep down, we believe we do as teachers.

On the next few pages are some of the things I keep in mine...

Ponder Point...

Is the answer to today's education problems giving every child access to a personal computer? If not, what is the answer? One might well ask what is education? Its oldest pedagogical meaning was to 'draw out' something latent or potential. But with the advent of globalisation and information superhighways, this conception is giving way to the the idea that education is about learning skills to access information, rather than developing the human personality.

Teachers, however, are not so easily put off course. Education is about the full development of the human personality, an inner voyage aimed at developing understanding and values, not just finding information.

Seen in this light, teachers are clearly at the heart of the education process. Without them, education is impossible. Many of them around the world are using the most creative techniques to open up children's minds and release the treasure within - the full potential of the individual.

UNESCO- Preface to the World Conference on Education for All

The Walnut

A conveniently sized reminder of the way the two hemispheres of the brain are linked together. There is more about this on page 10.

I look at it and think 'How can the lesson I am planning best appeal to the brain's need for system and structure, whilst allowing space for intuition?'

Generally this involves making sure the students see the point of the lesson and recognise how it fits with what we've done and what we're going to do.

It means making sure that learners who need to understand how bits of the subject operate get the information and practice they need.

It also means using lots of pictures, colours, exercises of imagination, and music, to give value and opportunity to right hemisphere learning. See page 89 onwards for some more practical pointers on how to do this.

The Business Card

This card (or certificate) has got my name - with lots of professional letters behind it. I've worked long and hard for those qualifications (and so have you). Those letters stand behind us when we introduce ideas which are new to the class, and reassure us that we know what we are doing - and why. We are professionals, and there are other people who think in the same way and support our judgment.

My business card doesn't say "teacher is always right", but it does say "teacher is part of a properly constituted, well-trained profession with high standards and has at least a reasonable chance of being right!"

The Bar of Soap

The sense of smell has direct access to the brain, which is why smells can be so instantly and powerfully evocative of past situations. My little bar of soap is lavender - and refreshingly whisks me to a sunny cottage garden.

What smell/fragrance takes you immediately to somewhere you want to be? How will you symbolise it in your treasure chest?

But that is only part of its role. It represents all the senses - the 'big ones' that we expect to cater for in a lesson, sight and sound for the visual and auditory learners (for more on learning styles see page 38) - plus touch and taste, and a reminder about movement. So I look for ways to bring them into the classroom through pictures, music, flowers, things to handle, little sweets as rewards, drinking water available.
I'm not saying that all of these are easy to bring in to every classroom situation, but you see the point and will adapt it for yourself.

Postcard

This is a Van Gogh self-portrait. You probably know the one. Fur hat...pipe smoking...right ear heavily bandaged. The lost ear is the important bit. The card was given to me by a participant on a seminar some years ago with the cryptic message **'Keep listening to 'em'.'**

I hope (but I'm not sure) it was given as an encouragement to keep on listening to student views, suggestions, experiences, input, feedback. Just in case it was a subtle prod to do **more** of that the postcard earns its place in the treasure chest, and I pick it up with slightly mixed feelings and a twinge of self-examination.

Jumping Frog

The little wooden frog is brightly coloured - red, green, orange, yellow, with a big grin. In my Treasure Chest he represents fun and games. He (I'm sure he's a 'he' because of the tie) is a very active character. He looks cheerful and positive and is a reminder to me of the importance of laughter in class, and of not taking things (myself included) too seriously!

Also his arms and legs dance, which is a nice stretch break reminder !

There's some brain gym and a stretch break example (Mr. Wriggle) on page 121.

Shining Star

It's not easy to achieve, but wouldn't it be great if each person in each class felt themselves - at least for a moment - to be a 'star'. One way and another there is a lot about the brain's limbic system, emotional intelligence, and self-esteem sprinkled through this book. This is because I'm sure that unless people feel good about themselves and what they are doing their learning is seriously limited.

One value of pair work is that it gives the partners opportunity to help each other - and being able to help another person is very good for a 'star quality' feeling.

Some schools of thought consider that giving praise suggests that something is better than expected, and therefore subconsciously establishes a low ceiling of expectation when it should be taken for granted that the learner should and will do brilliantly. Surely, though, we all flourish through being appreciated, don't we?

The teacher has the task of balancing praise, where deserved, with sensitive correction and not making anyone feel excluded. Very tricky, but as I explain later this is probably the key factor!

Throat Sweets

Voice energy carries a direct and powerful message. It can inspire and motivate a class - or drain and deaden it.

Sometimes the poor old teacher feels all wrung out and struggles to maintain concentration.

In a similar situation driving a car you might suck a sweet 'to raise blood sugar levels' and give a boost of energy. The same will work in class, but throat sweets have added value - they refresh a vital communication channel between teacher and students.

Look after your voice! If I know I'll need to raise it a lot with a particular group, or have a text to read, or something very important to put across then I so some voice warm ups (see page 120) as I go to work or walk down the corridor.

People may look at you as if you're crazy but if, at the end of the week, your voice is still fresh and working for you - who cares ?

Baboushka Pen

A while ago, on a trip to Russia, I was given a ballpoint pen encased in wood - painted with flowers and with a little 'grandma' figure on top. (It's not as complicated as it sounds.) It's not actually a fantastically good biro - quite ordinary in fact, but it works and it looks very attractive. When it comes out of the Treasure Chest I think *'Ordinary biro...but someone has taken the trouble to decorate it and make it special, and so it's nice to use it'*.

Ordinary biro - but decorated, so it's special. *Ordinary* grammar lesson... *ordinary* Friday test... *ordinary* staff meeting ... *ordinary* class worksheet...

Bendy Man

When you list the attributes of a successful (and surviving) teacher, high on the list must come...well, the Bendy man in the Treasure Chest has it.

A thin wire frame inside his rubbery body means you can move his limbs in all directions; he can stand or sit or twist into wonderfully contorted poses. He is FLEXIBLE.

Circumstances are always changing. Have you been in a situation recently where a bit more flexibility would have helped? In school a colleague is away and you are asked to cover at short notice. A new Department Head arrives with different requirements. In a lesson the students are finding things too easy (or too hard, or not interesting) and a quick change of plan is needed. These things cause great stress unless we are prepared to adapt to meet the new situation.

Bendy man is great. Because he isn't rigid he can't be broken. He may finish up after all these contortions in exactly the same position he started from, but that's a traveller's story...

Elephant

Rather chipped, and the trunk's broken off. The tiny soapstone elephant fits into the palm of one hand and has no commercial value. However, in Treasure Chest terms it represents two important learning points.

The first, obviously enough, is that *'an elephant never forgets'*. Along with teaching our subject, we need constantly to be teaching study skills. What guidance does the learner need to transfer information effectively from short to long-term memory? See page 43.

More sentimentally - but very importantly for me - this particular elephant was a gift from some young students. When later I visited their country and saw how little there was in the shops to live on let alone for children to buy as a present, the elephant took on a whole new significance. Have you ever received a present like this?

I look in the Treasure Chest now and feel that we teachers are giving all the time - but quite often we receive something precious from our students.

Garter

This is of frilly scarlet lace, with a little black silk bow, and is designed to hold up stockings (or rather, as I only have one, a stocking). I'm not sure why I have only one, or where it originally came from (my wife certainly denies any knowledge of it) but in Treasure Chest terms it symbolises *SUPPORT*. The support the teacher gives to the learners, that learners give to each other and, ideally, that they also give to the teacher.

Supportive comments, supportive criticism, supportive pair and group work...and supportive colleagues. Teaching can be such a lonely business once you are inside that classroom. It's *very* lonely if things aren't going well or you feel that you are the only person trying to introduce new ideas. Look for individuals or networks to share your worries – and successes – with. Everyone needs some support!

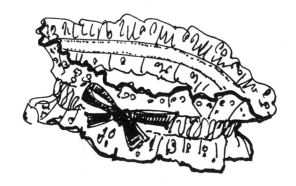

Jet Plane

I suppose that whatever subject we teach we are all trying to enable our students to fly faster and higher than they imagined possible and, above all, to fly the plane for themselves!

My model plane has wheels for getting off the ground and swing wings that fold back into a very streamline shape as speed increases. The model plane is about learner independence. How do we encourage students to get the skills they need to work on their own?

We may achieve this by way of introducing study skills (there's more on this on page 43) or activities which lead to discussion about how to learn, or by teaching something specific e.g. the phonetic alphabet to language learners so they can look up the pronunciation of new words in a dictionary. Try 'The cat in the tree' as an example of linking items. It's on page 49.

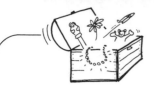

Bead Necklace

The beads are blue and (possibly) coral, and there are lots of them. Rather pretty. That's not really why they are in the Treasure Chest though. My attention is on the thread, which is very fine and looks extremely fragile.

It's in the nature of longish necklaces to get tangled. The beads get snarled up in horrid tangles and the thread seems inextricably knotted.

In the class we have individual people all linked by the fact of learning - having to learn - together. Relationships can get tangled.

An important part of the teacher's 'authority' - the establishing of a good learning atmosphere and the building of a learning community - is to look out for these potentially damaging tangles, and patiently to work on sorting them out ensuring that the fragile thread doesn't break!

The Packet of Seeds

Terms, courses, classes, school years seem to have flown by when we look back at them, but at the time they can seem very drawn out and unrewarding. We commit ourselves to doing the best we can (circumstances considered) and then we do a bit more because we're the sort of people we are - and we care. Day by day, week by week we give out information, ideas, creativity, opportunities. Sometimes classes are unreceptive and unappreciative, but we do our best - planting the seeds, watering them, tending them and...sometimes...wondering *'Why am I doing this?' 'Why bother?'*

And then, unexpectedly, a seed begins to germinate - later, perhaps, a flower blooms. Someone discovers *for herself* an interest in the subject. Someone gets a job because of a skill they've learned from you, or an exam they've passed because of your encouragement. Sometimes a whole bouquet of flowers will surround you with colour and fragrance. After all, which of us can't identify a teacher who had a positive influence on our development and life choices?

The packet of seeds in my Treasure Chest are Nigella, but I prefer their common name 'Love-in-the mist'. We faithfully tend the seeds, often in the mist, thinking we don't really know the way. Then sometimes, just sometimes, it's suddenly Springtime!

Then we do know why we are teachers, and we do know why we bother, and we do know it's the most important job in the world. And then we should pause a moment, smile with pleasure at what has happened, and give ourselves a very big pat on the back. We deserve it !

"No one ever forgets a good teacher!"

Challenge

There were 14 items in my Treasure Chest. Can you complete the illustrations? Then add some of your own?

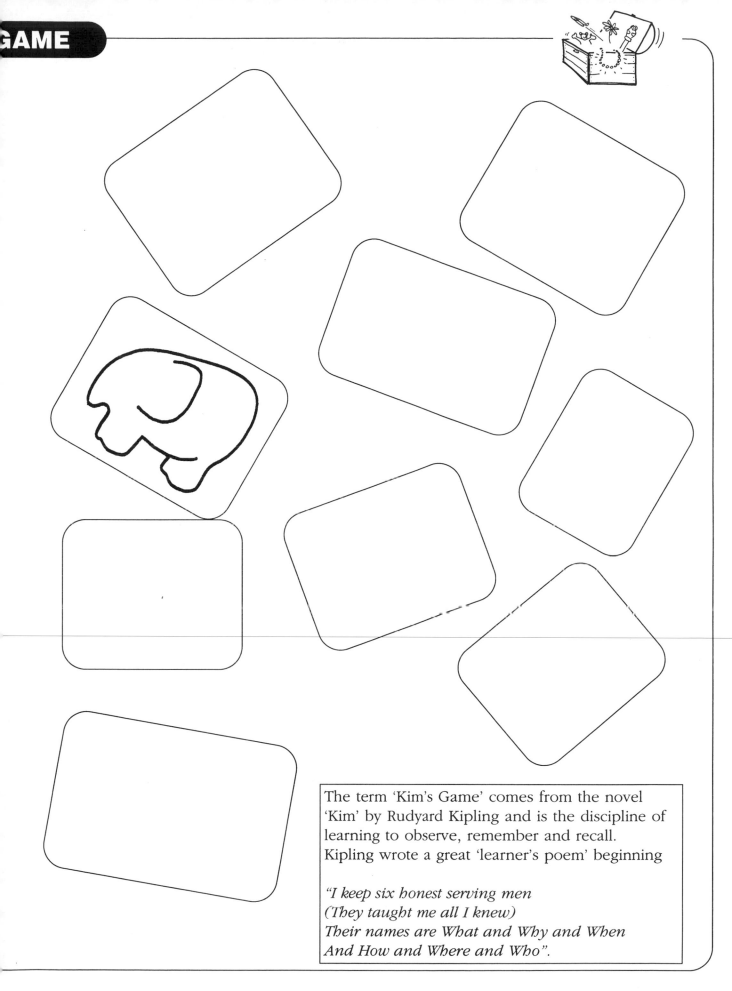

The term 'Kim's Game' comes from the novel 'Kim' by Rudyard Kipling and is the discipline of learning to observe, remember and recall.
Kipling wrote a great 'learner's poem' beginning

"I keep six honest serving men
(They taught me all I knew)
Their names are What and Why and When
And How and Where and Who".

TAKE A BREATHER TIME!

If you have been reading *Teaching for Success*

for the last twenty minutes or longer

You deserve a break!

Have a stretch / a little walk around / something to drink....

Ponder Point...

"All over the world there is a big concern about the education system. I think the most important transformation we can start is to add an additional subject from Kindergarten to colleges directed to teaching the development of the right and the left brain. We have to continue teaching maths, biology, chemistry, physics and so on, but in addition why don't we start teaching in a formal way how to develop human intelligence and human capacity for loving? If we have a method for continually activating and using our brain, we are going to live more, and live better. I'm sure that the best ideal for a person is to die young - as late as possible!"

Louis Machado – formerly Minister for the Development of Human Intelligence, Venezuela

Learning Styles – and Memory

Ponder Point...

Pause for a moment to watch the hill farmer remaking a dry-stone wall. Rough stones are chosen, lifted, fitted together without any mortar. You hear the 'clunk' as one stone is brought into contact with another. It's slow, careful, patient, work - long flat stones for strength, heavy, chunky stones to anchor them, smaller stones to be wedged in and give stability.

Now turn quickly to the nearby stream that splashes and rushes down through deep pools and craggy falls. The water churns in a flurry of foam. A great salmon, driven by instinct, battles its way from the sea to the river where it was born, leaping in a bright flash of silver over the falls to the clear water beyond.

Such a contrast. The salmon, all flashing energy and speed. The craftsman with quiet judgment and infinite patience. Two ways of working. We can only recognise their differentness, and their rightness.

Learning styles

The commonly identified learning styles are **Visual** - the need to see something either written or in picture form, or as a picture in the mind. **Auditory** - to be able to hear a satisfyingly clear signal. This will usually be voice, but could be in conjunction with music or natural sounds. **Kinaesthetic** - the need physically to move in response to a task, which might mean acting, demonstrating, doing something with the learning (or teaching) material - or might just mean doodling or wriggling, or walking around. Taste and smell have powerful brain connections and can instantly impact on the limbic system in a positive or negative way. We should not neglect the importance of the **Olfactory** or **Gustatory** systems, but they are generally less apparent in the classroom than the other three.

It is very uncommon to come across a student who is solely a visual or an auditory or a kinaesthetic learner. I think I've met one - a language student who took no notes at all during an intensive course and, as far as I could see, didn't read anything either, but made remarkable progress by having a truly astonishing 'ear' for language. The more common reality is that we all operate a number of systems but often have a preference for one (which may change at different stages of life or times of the day).

Observing eye movements can give you a clue to how people are processing thoughts. See page 59 for examples of this.

Mis-match between a student's preferred learning styles and the dominant way information is presented will set up all sorts of barriers (see *limbic system*) and we should strive to present a package so comprehensive that no one will feel excluded. Here I must apologise to everyone reading this linear text who would be happier *listening* to a dramatised version on cassette, *piecing it together* as a jigsaw, or slowly *chewing it !*

WHAT KIND OF LEARNER ARE YOU?

Having succeeded well enough with our own education to qualify as a teacher - and to want to teach - we are likely to have developed our own learning strategies and the ability to 'receive' information in a number of ways. When I talk to teachers my impression is that most have an idea of their learning preference - visual, auditory, kinaesthetic - and that most **say** they would **see** themselves **feel** that their preferences fluctuate. My 'research' on this is purely anecdotal but indicates a much higher proportion of strongly kinaesthetic learners amongst primary school teachers than amongst secondary school teachers. As younger learners especially need and enjoy lots of movement, this may be a case of personal learning style leading to a career path?

The questionnaire that follows is a not-very-scientific 'awareness raiser'. Before you do it, jot down your present view of your preferred learning style - kinaesthetic, visual, auditory.

I think I am, primarily, a _____ learner.

I see what you mean ...

I don't feel right ...

I hear what you say ...

Now do the quiz. I'm not maintaining that the quiz will always be a more accurate guide than your current opinion, only that it might usefully challenge some assumptions!

WHAT KIND OF LEARNER ARE YOU?

Do the quiz very quickly - first reactions only - then look on the page opposite.

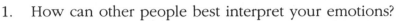

1. How can other people best interpret your emotions?
   a. through your facial expressions
   b. from the quality of your voice
   c. through your general body language

2. How do you manage to keep up with current events?
   a. by reading the newspaper thoroughly when you have the time
   b. by listening to the radio or watching the TV news
   c. by quickly reading the paper or spending just a few minutes watching the TV news

3. What sort of driver (or passenger) are you?
   a. you frequently check the rear view mirror and watch the road carefully
   b. you turn on the radio as soon as you get into the car
   c. you can't get comfortable in the seat and continually shift position

4. How do you prefer to conduct business?
   a. by having face-to-face meetings or writing letters, faxes, emails etc.
   b. over the phone because it saves time
   c. by talking while you are walking, jogging or doing something else physical

5. How do you behave at meetings?
   a. you come prepared with notes and displays
   b. you enjoy discussing issues and hearing other points of view
   c. you spend a lot of your time doodling

6. Which do you prefer doing in your free time?
   a. watching TV or going to the cinema
   b. listening to the radio, going to a concert or playing a musical instrument
   c. engaging in a physical activity of some kind

7. What is your instant response to the word 'horse'. Do you
   a. see a horse?
   b. hear a horse?
   c. feel the sensation of patting, grooming or riding a horse?

8. Your school has surprisingly given you a budget to improve your classsroom.
   Is your priority to ensure a good
   a. white board and lots of excellent wall posters?
   b. CD/cassette player plus microphone?
   c. Comfortable and easily rearranged tables and chairs?

Adapted from **Who are you?** Michael Berman *English Experience*

Your Score
Count up your number of
    a –
    b –
    c –

What your score may mean...

*Mostly **a***
As a visual learner yourself you will probably use the board a lot, have pictures on the classroom walls, use visual aids and expect students to take a lot of notes. You like to see well-presented student work.

*Mostly **b***
Being an auditory learner yourself you will give a lot of verbal instructions and expect students to keep quiet to listen. You will probably use a cassette player, encourage discussions and pay a lot of attention to the way students give opinions.

*Mostly **c***
Because, as a kinaesthetic learner yourself, you like to move around and do things, you will organise your classroom, as far as possible, to allow students to do this too. You will like using group activities and encourage students to the front to put things on the board or demonstrate what they've learned.

Of course, almost everyone - and certainly most teachers - include a mixture of learning styles in their behaviour. But two questions we have to ask are,

"Is my teaching style clearly determined by my own learning style?"

"Are there students in any of my classes who are blocked because they just don't receive information in that way?"

Challenge

To look at each lesson and see that it contains opportunities for kinaesthetic, auditory, and visual learners to *grasp, register, take in* the key information.

WHAT A GREAT MEMORY!

Remembering doesn't happen in one way only, nor is memory stored in one place. It's a multi-purpose, many-layered business, and the more routes and reinforcements (encoding) which we bring into play, the higher the likelihood that information will transfer from *short* to *long term* memory. The transfer is, after all, an important part of what we are, as teachers, trying to help our students accomplish.

This on-going question of "how the transfer takes place" is the great undiscussed question in staff rooms around the world. It is actually what teaching and learning is about - but pressures of syllabus and timetable planning, preparation for tomorrow, the heap of marking and so on constantly push it to the bottom of the pile. So let's "flag it" as a key issue and start with ourselves.

Thank you for taking the task seriously. Everything which follows will have more meaning now as you will relate it to your own experience.

Challenge

This space is for 5 minutes of intra-personal examination and scribbling of notes. *How do I remember things ?*

If you possibly can, brainstorm the same question with colleagues. You'll be surprised at the wide variety of approaches people use. Every time I've done this activity I've been amazed at the learning techniques colleagues have developed, and that for some people the things that I take for granted are completely new.

The point is obvious. Time and time again, I ask students '*What have you learned about learning at school?*' The response is generally a moment of non-comprehension followed by '*We learned history, and mathematics, and French, and Information Technology......but we never did anything about 'Learning'!*'

The essential question of how to help students take enthusiastic and appropriate responsibility for the skill of learning is very rarely addressed because it is not yet a subject on most timetables (a situation which needs to be changed). Teaching it is therefore nobody's particular responsibility.

On the page opposite is a modest scheme of approaches which most frequently come up in the "How I learn" discussion. Just as in a teachers' group, individuals will have their own favourite methods, so, in a class, not everything will work for everyone.

SHORT-TERM TO LONG-TERM MEMORY

Voices of the learners are in italics.

Personal significance... What is my motivation for learning this? What will it help me to do? *I need to establish the payoff. I'll be able to ski/speak German/answer a question on...* NB Beware of very generalised motivation (To pass my exams). The more specific the significance the better (There's a good chance there'll be a question on the Great Lakes in my Geography exam, so it's a good investment to spend 10 minutes learning the names in order of size.)

Repetition... *Recycling... Going over it again next day... Doing the same thing in a different way.* As teachers I think we often get two things wrong. One is to underestimate the brain's ability to work out the meaning of what it wants to know. The other is to underestimate the number of 'meetings' with new information which are necessary before it is 'learned' (transferred to long-term memory). The trend is always for pressure on the timetable to increase. More and more information. Higher and higher standards. The danger is that we'll find ourselves throwing increasing quantities of mud at the wall in the hope that some of it will stick. It's likely that, as learners, we have to encounter information about four times before it 'sticks'.

Using pictures... *Linking words/ideas to pictures... Visualising situations in my mind.* Most of us have powerful visual memories - actual pictures and pictures in the mind's eye, the product of imagination. Pictures often precede words in recall from memory. See the exercise on page 49.

...and using colour. Each time we use a coloured felt tip/highlighter it sends a 'notice this' signal to the brain as well as making a deliberate connection between the learner and the page. The page becomes more interesting to look at and develops its own character for when the time comes to revise. As an example of the systematic use of colour for clarification see Paula the Painter. (page 92)

Imitation... *I learn best by watching someone else and then copying what they do!* Peer group teaching is powerful.

Sorting... *Getting my notes in order... Putting things on cards and playing 'Memory'... Using a learning card box and moving the cards to a different compartment as I learn them.* There is, for most people, an innate, if unfulfilled, desire to categorise things, to put like with like, to know where to find things. Time spent checking that students know how to keep notes in a filing system that actually works for them (on disk, in a folder, a card system or whatever) is well spent. Likewise activities which involve sorting, matching, and ordering are 'BRAIN-*friendly*'.

Drama/movement... *I act things out... I can't sit still and learn, I have to walk around.* We can hear the voice of the kinaesthetic learner.

Music/relaxation... *Rock music cuts out all interference. I don't notice it when I'm working ... I do some breathing and yoga exercises to get myself ready for learning ... When I'm listening to classical music I'm calmer, I don't get frustrated, I concentrate longer.*
There's more on the classroom application of music on page 115.

Linking... *I put things into stories because it's easy to remember a story.* We connect what is new to what we already know. If there's a link of information missing it's much easier to find it if we remember what goes either side of it in a story. There is a demonstration of this on page 49.

Mnemonics... another form of linking... **R**ichard **of Y**ork **g**ave **b**attle **in v**ain (colours of the rainbow– red orange yellow green blue indigo violet) What others do you know? The planets? Musical notation?

Concentration spans... *I make sure I take regular breaks to keep my concentration. ... I have a drink of water and maybe a biscuit or banana every half hour.* Concentration begins to flag after a certain time particularly if we're sitting over a desk, or there are distractions. Rather than fight it we need a short break (a Mr Wriggle - page 121) and refreshment. I used to advocate water and fruit - but having read two research articles recently claiming that chewing gum is good for the brain (and coffee is good for the heart) maybe one can't be too proscriptive!

Humour...   Laughter is a reflex apparently involving the simultaneous involuntary contraction of fifteen facial muscles. Healthy laughter is a sharing moment, but additionally, things which strike us as funny because they are bizarre, force together unexpected images and because of their incongruity 'stick' in the memory. The odder, more comical, more personal, and quite often it seems, the ruder the associations, the more likely they are to be encoded.

Review before sleep... As we fall asleep our brain wave patterns change. Reading through key notes before sleep we are physically and mentally relaxed. The brain is open to the signal 'I'm reading this because it's important. Please do some work on it while I'm asleep!'

The brain is very used to this - it naturally shuffles and sorts the stimuli of the day (the rapid eye movement of a sleeping child). If you don't already use this technique, try it and test yourself at breakfast!

Ponder Point...

We are looking for more than a mechanical application of selected techniques. We are looking to achieve success which will encourage confidence and lead to a real eagerness to learn - *a disposition for learning*.   (Professor Lilian Katz)

When my own children came to their big exam revision stage, the eldest discovered mind maps and made huge flip charts which covered his wall with intricate spidery patterns. This worked very well for him and in due course he enthusiastically sold the idea to younger brother at exam time. Result, frustration. Younger brother discovered he learned best by lying on the floor to revise (with pop music hammering through the stereo headphones). Naturally, younger sister was presented with both these strategies, and rapidly found that they didn't work for her. She needed to walk up and down, up and down (often all night) book open in hand reading aloud and discussing with herself.

The point is that unless teachers draw attention to different possibilities and encourage students to experiment, the deep-rooted idea that "working hard = sitting at a desk for four hours" may be the only model that some students (and their parents) ever recognise.

QUICK RECAP

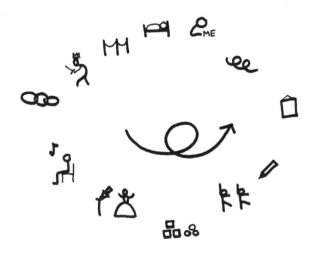

What do they represent?

Our artist has forgotten to illustrate one of the memory pointers! Which one is missing?

MEMORY TEST

Before you start this test make sure you have a **watch**. You will also need a **blank piece of paper** and a **pen** for later. Give yourself **exactly 2 minutes** to learn these words. Don't cheat. Stop after 2 minutes.
YOU MUST NOT WRITE ANYTHING DOWN.

flower
fork
love
sheep
radio
fence
blue
book
stream
wisdom
table
fork
bird
memory
paper
tree
grass
stream
carbon paper
truth
cat
pen
spaceman
knife
desk

Challenge

Close the book. Take the blank paper. Give yourself exactly **one minute** to write the words on the blank paper.

Assuming you have stuck to the rules and are now checking your score, welcome back!

Sorry about the 'Sergeant Major'-type instructions. How did you do?

If you remembered ten or more you probably had a **strategy**. What was it?

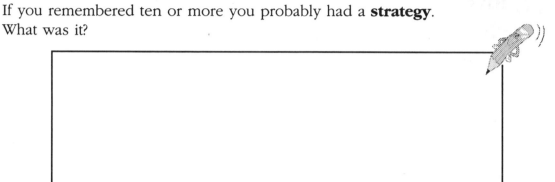

How many of the words do you think you would remember if you were suddenly asked to do the test again in a month's time?

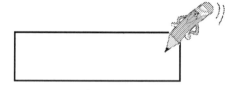

Of course, the activity is set up in a very loaded way.

The MEMORY TEST is set with no context. No reason to do it is given. There is no encouragement, just several bald instructions.

People with well-developed learning strategies (successful learners themselves - quite often teachers) will find a way to tackle the task, but others will be thrown by the implied pressure of a timed test. *(Will I fail? Maybe my memory is worse than average...)*

Would it help to have a more multi-style presentation? Read on...

Here's a story which contains 25 key words. Some of the words occur twice (in which case they count as two words). It's an easy story to remember. Read it aloud.

There's a **tree**. There's a **cat** (miaow) in the tree and the cat is in **love** with a **bird** (tweet tweet). Under the tree is a **table** with a **knife** and a **fork** - and another **fork**! There's a **desk**. On it there's a **book** about our subject, **memory**. There's also **paper**, a **pen** and **carbon paper**. Near the desk is a **sheep** eating **grass** and thinking about **TRUTH** and **WISDOM**. Wheeee....here comes a **spaceman** with a **radio** and a **blue flower**. (Smell it...beautiful...) Let's jump over the **fence**. *Splash!* We're in a **stream** and *splash*, we're in another **stream**!

Challenge

Check again. Write out the 25 words on a blank piece of paper. Is there a significant improvement in your score?

"The cat in the tree" is not called a 'test'. It contains the same information load but is presented with items clustered in groups, and a story with various "sense stimulators."

For most people, the second approach will be much easier, and with a couple of repetitions (and the addition of some Do-it-Yourself *colour*, and some *gestures/movements*) will ensure that all 25 words (it's much easier to check when the target is defined) are transferred into long-term memory.

Tests, of course, can concentrate the mind wonderfully and provide a strong motive for learning (which is not the same as providing an effective **way** of learning)

The linking into a story, the use of visuals, the sound effects, and colouring, and funny gestures, and positive encouragement are only *a part* of the purpose of this activity. So please jot down the words again now...

...then, when you're ready, check again with the picture (or the story).

 ——————————————————————————— **Challenge**

Identify any words you **didn't** recall. Think to yourself *'why did I miss those?'* and work out your *own strategy* for remembering (encoding) them next time.

The objective is to encourage 'learners' to take responsibility for developing their own learning skills. (This relates to the jet plane in the Treasure Chest page 31.)

MEMORY
The limbic link with emotion

Tell me everything about your first day at school!

"I can't remember that far back!"

Let's approach it a different way....

Let's remember some very early things about school...

As you answer these questions, let some **pictures** or **sounds** or **smells** come into your mind. Allow several seconds for an image to develop and stabilise. Ideally, do this exercise in a comfortable place, with relaxing music, and where you know you won't be interrupted.

★ Where were you living when you first went to school?

★ Can you visualise your house or apartment?

★ Did you have sisters or brothers at school?

★ How did you go there? On foot? By bus? In a car?

★ Did you wear any special uniform?

★ Did you have lunch there, or did you come home?

★ What was the school like? Is your impression of an old building or a new one?

★ Do you see it as a light and open building, or dark and closed?

★ Was there a grass playing field? or a playground?

★ Do you remember it as a noisy or a quiet place?

★ Did you sit at desks in rows, or at little tables?

★ Does the school have a special smell that you remember?

★ What sounds do you especially remember?

★ Was your first teacher a lady or a man?

★ Old?... Young?... Kind?... Strict?

★ When you started school what things did you like about it?

★ What things didn't you like about school?

★ Did you have lots of friends, or did you feel a bit lonely?

Focus a picture of the very young 'You' at school for a moment. Now, talk aloud – to a partner (or to yourself) about your early school experiences.

I CAN REMEMBER THAT FAR BACK!

If, at the beginning of the exercise, you thought *'I can't remember that far back'* you had a fairly typical reaction! Even at the moment of the *'Now share with your neighbour...'* lots of people feel *'I haven't got anything to say'*. Almost invariably once participants begin to speak, however uncertainly, about the pictures in their memory those pictures become clearer and words begin to flow. One picture triggers another. Because beginning school is an important experience, and an emotional one, it is multi-referenced in the brain.

Some points to note

1. As with all Guided Visualisations involving feelings, care should be taken to keep the subject matter positive. Avoid anything which could raise disturbing memories. There is more on visualisation on page 96.

2. As a matter of interest, carry out a poll with colleagues who have also done this visualisation. How many of your group have, broadly speaking, a positive memory of early school and how many have, in general, a negative memory? Having done this exercise with hundreds of teachers in many different countries, my highly unscientific appraisal is that between half and two-thirds of people have basically positive memories - which leaves a lot who don't!

3. Whatever has emotional impact is remembered. This doesn't mean that every lesson on the Atomic table or the Past Perfect Tense has to finish up looking like the final Act of 'Hamlet'.

As we see in the Tango of Learning on page 60 – Self-investment – that feeling of making a valuable contribution and being given credit – is the answer.

Challenge

How can you make sure that the learners you know get off to a positive start to their schooling and maintain their high level of self-esteem?

Mind Map Review

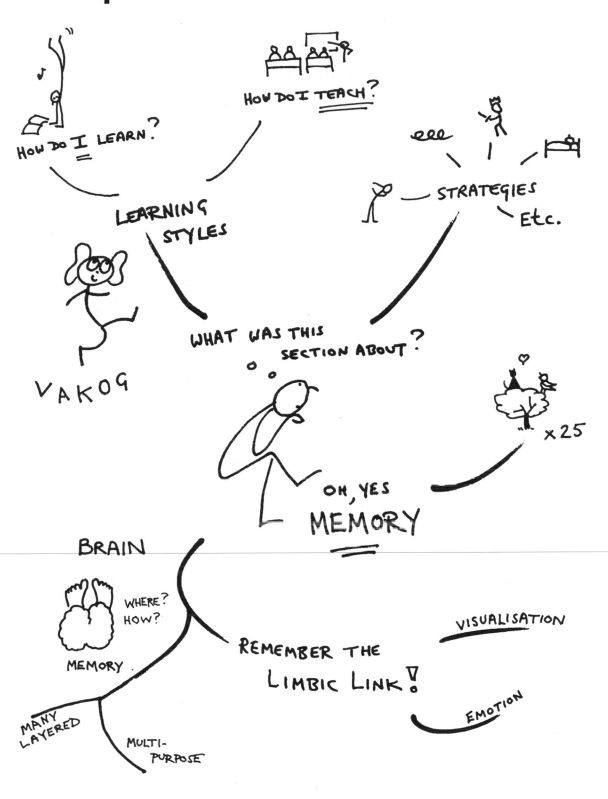

Contributions to teaching which draw their inspiration from excitement about our amazing brain

Ponder Point...

A thought on suggestopedia which applies to all teaching

"Dr. Lozanov saw his aim as not just the teaching of languages but the *tapping of the reserve capacity of the brain;* in other words, the development of potential.

In following him along this path and venturing even further along it, we are doing more than just improving learning and teaching methods. We are showing both students and teachers how the classroom can be *a place of excitement and fulfilment, a place where unsuspected talents and interests are discovered, visions of a better future glimpsed and relationships deepened.*"

Michael Lawlor, Co-Founder and Past President of SEAL

Affective Approaches

SOME TERMS

Holistic (Wholistic) Learning

Concerned with the whole person involving mind, body and spirit.

Affective

Concerning the emotions. One aim of affective approaches is to counterbalance the emphasis placed on exclusively intellectual learning.

Right and Left Brain

Since the Nobel Prize-winning work of Sperry and Ornstein in the 1960s there has been great emphasis on the function of different areas of the brain in relation to learning. Normally the left hemisphere of the brain processes analytically whilst the right hemisphere responds to music, art and spatial relationships. This is a useful – although very simplified – approximation (see page 10). The application of BRAIN-*friendly* techniques seeks to involve both hemispheres actively – and other areas as well.

Triune Brain

Looked at in cross section this simple model of the brain identifies three major developments of the brain in evolutionary terms – The Reptilian brain (reflex, systems maintenance), the limbic system (emotions, memory), and the cerebral cortex (intellect). It should be borne in mind that the brain is enormously complex, and whilst understanding of it is improving all the time, there is still a long way to go.

Brainwaves and Mind/body Harmony

Physical brainwaves and activity in different parts of the brain can be measured and shown visually on screen or print-outs. For convenience, different bands of activity are given different names. (Reading this you are in a Beta state. If you fall asleep you are in Delta – and I am failing to communicate!)

Various learning approaches place great importance on brainwave states – the **Alpha state** in particular, where the brain seems to receive information without conscious processing. This ideal receptive learning state is physically relaxed, with no stress or posture-induced tension. The person is emotionally calm and mentally alert. Ways of achieving this state include sitting quietly listening to slow (typically Baroque) music, **Yoga** breathing and stretching exercises, and **Autogenic training**, whereby tensing and relaxing the muscles systematically around the body induces a deep level of relaxation.

Humanistic Psychology

Psychology deriving from a modern (1960s onwards) concern with self-awareness and personal development. The evidence of this thinking might be seen in teaching where:
● Attention is given to the purposes of the learner, his/her interests and needs
● The autonomy, responsibility and creativity of the learner is an important factor in the 'balance of power' in the class
● The teacher sees the subject as engaging the learner not only intellectually but affectively as well.

Educational Kinesiology (Edu-K) – Brain Gym

Physical exercises designed to encourage better hemispheric (see Left-Right Brain) integration, and so improve learning. Students report enhanced abilities in visual and auditory perception and improved motor skills. It is especially valuable for children who have difficulties learning to learn. More on this on page 121.

Mind maps (Radiant Thinking)

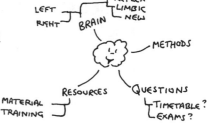

A non-linear method of note taking which links key words and ideas. Pioneered by Tony Buzan, who has done much to introduce and popularise study skills such as memory training and speed reading. More on this on page 99.

Multiple Intelligence Theory

An important and holistic effort to break the mould of evaluating intelligence solely by narrow linguistic or mathematically based I.Q. tests. Howard Gardner establishes the case for recognising and valuing at least eight important intelligences (logical-mathematical, linguistic, musical, spatial, kinaesthetic, interpersonal, intrapersonal, naturalist). More on this on page 64.

Emotional Intelligence

As with Multiple Intelligence, there is an issue about whether intelligence can be satisfactorily defined, especially in brain terms. However, the importance of emotions, feelings, the affective in learning is not in doubt, and there is much more on this on page 69.

Instrumental Enrichment

The work of Reuven Feuerstein * strikes a further blow at the concept of a fixed IQ. By providing strategies for teaching socially and genetically handicapped children how to think more effectively, he demonstrates that in the 'Nature v. Nurture' debate, the plasticity of the brain can to a great extent compensate for apparent disadvantages and that we are not 'prisoners of our genes'.

Total Physical Response

Language learning in a very supportive group dynamic through movement and gestures. Learners absorb and assimilate information by responding to commands which the teacher models. Developed by James Asher. **

Changing Children's Minds Howard Sharron Souvenir Press ISBN 0 285 65034 a book for those interested in Feuerstein's instrumental enrichment work.

** *Learning another language through actions* Sky Oak Productions, PO Box 1102, Los Gatos, California 95031 USA.

Visualising and Imaging

'Imaging' is making pictures in your mind, and Guided Visualisation usually means following a scripted journey of imagination to 'discover' an inner resource. The ingredients are part of everyday life. Sports personalities talk about 'visualising' a shot. Supermarkets, airlines, and dentists all use gentle music as an aid to relaxation.

There are several examples of what I call 'visualisation ladders' in this book (page 97, for example).

Suggestopedia

A method of instruction which fosters positive psychological growth in addition to imparting information. Learning is facilitated or inhibited by psychological or environmental factors. Get the 'internal' and 'external' right and the barriers are removed. Learning takes place at levels other than just the conscious. Developed by the Bulgarian doctor and psychotherapist Georgi Lozanov, it became known in the West in the 1970s.

Adaptations and more eclectic versions exist, but it was an interest in Lozanov's work that led to the formation of SEAL, the Society for Effective Affective Learning.

A Suggestopedic class is conducted according to a carefully researched cycle:

(Quotations in *italics* are from Dr. Lozanov's lectures.)

1 INTRODUCTION

'This creates a suitable environment for learning'. The subject matter is presented in a lively way by the teacher, using pictures, props, acting, mime, and involving the students.

2 THE SESSION

Active Concert. *'The linguistic aim is to put material into the memory through many moods, associations and channels'.* The teacher plays a tape of classical music and reads a text at the same time.

Passive Concert. This is a stage of concentrative psychological relaxation. *'The nervous system is calm but the brain is active, directing energy where it is most needed.'* The teacher reads with clear pronunciation, natural intonation, and at normal speed, to Baroque music.

3 ELABORATION

This practice phase is rich in games with specific teaching points, different ways of reading the text, songs, etc. *'All material must be elaborated globally – every part must be connected with another. Nothing should be done in isolation. This is the most difficult part'.*

I have based my own teaching for the past eight years on developing ideas from Suggestopedia. It works! It's a great experience for the learner and teacher – but not easy to describe! *Superlearning, Accelerated Learning,* BRAIN-*friendly Learning* are commercially patented terms indicating eclectic systems deriving from Suggestopedia though often linked to other learning approaches described here.

Suggestopedia features a supportive, positive atmosphere; use of Classical/Baroque music; games, songs, peripherals; texts written as dramas; ongoing role play; thorough reworking of target material. (See also the Suggestopedic Elephant on page 80)

Neuro-linguistic Programming

NLP is a set of guiding principles, attitudes and techniques that enable you to change or eliminate behaviour patterns as you wish. NLP describes the dynamics between the mind (neuro) and language (linguistic) and how their interplay 'programmes' our behaviour. It began in the early 1970s with Bandler and Grinder who explored how to model excellence by closely observing three highly successful therapists at work. They relied not only on what the therapists said they were doing, but on the patterns of language and behaviour they actually used. In short, NLP is about having the awareness and skills to know what motivates you and influences others.

The pillars of NLP are:

Rapport – with yourself and others
Outcomes – being clear about what you want
Sensory acuity – really noticing how things are (this includes trusting your intuition)
Flexibility – taking responsibility for your choices and being prepared to change

NLP posits a number of presuppositions.
One is that the mind and body are connected. For example, if you are feeling dejected this will show in your body language. By changing your posture - standing more upright, looking up, smiling, you will change your physiology and actually feel better.
Another is that 'the map is not the territory'. We each see the world through our own filters. Others will have a different map.

NLP proposes a four step basic action model
1 know what you want - set your objectives
2 Take action - plan something and do it. *We have all the resources we need'.*
3 Notice the response. *'The meaning of my communication is the response I get'.*
4 Respond to the response you get, remembering that *'there is no such thing as failure, only feedback.'*

One of the major contributions of NLP in education is to make teachers think more about VAKOG - the different learning styles (Visual Auditory Kinaesthetic Olfactory Gustatory) we looked at on page 38, and recognise that, for example, kinaesthetic learners may not just be 'messing about' if they are fidgeting when supposed to be writing - they actually **need** to move to learn. NLP suggests that it is possible to learn a good deal about how people are processing information by watching their eye movements. Here are typical examples...

Eye movements - illustrated as you look at someone's face

1. Looking up
- **visualising**

a. Remembering something.

*b. Imagining (constructing)
what something might be like.*

2. Looking sideways
- **processing auditorily**

a. Remembering something heard.

b. Imagining a sound..

3. Looking down
- **feeling... kinaesthetic...**

a. Recalling a bodily sensation ...

c. Recalling an emotion.

b. Recalling a taste

And .....

Remembering a smell

Challenge

Test the eye movement theory with a colleague.

Thinking skills

A vital aspect of an affective approach to making good use of the brain in learning. These skills are too often regarded and treated as a very 'left-brained' activity. As far as the brain is concerned, thinking is not something which happens automatically, like breathing. It can be developed, and improved. Higher order thinking skills, the ability to analyse and make connections, to reason, solve problems and think creatively are becoming recognised as crucial teaching concerns. Edward de Bono's practical work over many years on lateral thinking has contributed to this, as has Vygotsky's concept of providing children with mental tools which can be used independently and creatively to extend their abilities.

This interest in teaching thinking skills is being taken on by, for example, CASE- the Cognitive Acceleration through Science Education programme - created by professors Philip Adey and Michael Shayer of King's College, London.

Pre-conscious (or sub-conscious) processing

Picture the mind as an iceberg. Only a tiny part, the conscious mind, is 'visible' - those things we are aware of because we are aware of them! Psychologists such as Antonio Damasio suggest that most of what goes on in the mind/body complex happens below conscious awareness - the invisible 'bulk of the iceberg'. As teachers (and human beings) we will have an awareness of this, especially in relation to the limbic system, memory, and emotional intelligence. The issue of the brain and consciousness is, perhaps, 'the final frontier' for neuro-scientists. Certainly it is far too complex to go into here★.

★Read Damasio's
Descartes' error
or
Susan Greenfield's
The Human Brain

THE TANGO OF LEARNING!

You will notice that a considerable amount of what is described in Teaching for Success relates to the 'affective' – how we _feel_ about what is happening. In brain terms this depends on what is happening in the limbic system.

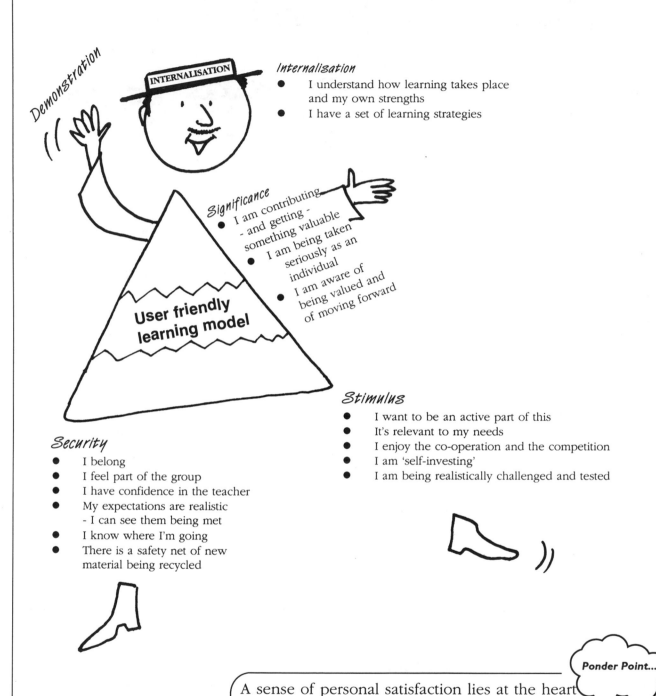

Demonstration

INTERNALISATION

Internalisation
- I understand how learning takes place and my own strengths
- I have a set of learning strategies

Significance
- I am contributing - and getting - something valuable
- I am being taken seriously as an individual
- I am aware of being valued and of moving forward

User friendly learning model

Stimulus
- I want to be an active part of this
- It's relevant to my needs
- I enjoy the co-operation and the competition
- I am 'self-investing'
- I am being realistically challenged and tested

Security
- I belong
- I feel part of the group
- I have confidence in the teacher
- My expectations are realistic - I can see them being met
- I know where I'm going
- There is a safety net of new material being recycled

Ponder Point...

A sense of personal satisfaction lies at the heart of successful learning. (Sir Christopher Ball)

THE LEARNING ENVIRONMENT

Broadly speaking there are two inter-connected 'environments'. The *external* physical situation and the *internal* 'affective' how-we-feel situation. The teacher has the task of attempting to make both environments positive. The external may present difficulties but is at least visible. Is the room as interesting and comfortable for working as it can be? What's on the walls? Is there welcoming music? Can everyone see the board? Does the seating arrangement allow students as well as teacher to move? Is there some way (work displayed/items contributed) by which students feel the room 'belongs' to them? Is there enough oxygen? Is it warm, cool, bright, shady enough? Does the room look 'cared for'? The external learning environment also encompasses the opportunity to learn through the provision of adequate resources.

The 'internal' learning environment is affected by the external. Do I (student or teacher) feel cheered or depressed by this room? The internal learning environment is, of course, much more subtle, and affected by many other factors. Both the 'Tango of Learning' and the 'Chinese vase' (page 62) explore this area of 'feelings'. So too, Explorer 4 in the Suggestopedic Elephant describes the barriers to learning which manifest themselves as poor motivation, resentment, sense of inadequacy. Feelings of unease, embarrassment, anxiety - not being able to see the point of a lesson, poor relationships with peer group, teacher, family - these and other factors contribute to a brain state which prioritises 'fight or flight' above 'focus on learning'.

Successful learning is most likely if the learner:
a. has high confidence and good self-esteem
b. is strongly motivated to learn and
c. is able to learn in an environment characterised by
   'high challenge' coupled with 'low threat'.

Internal & External environments affect each other.

My experience of teaching in prisons is very limited and I have great admiration for those who do. An observation, albeit a generalisation, is that the prison learning environment is about as un-brain-friendly as can be. Where I worked was hot, stuffy, airless (makes for lethargy) and the walls an energy-sapping sludge-brown pink. The clanging gates, shouted instructions, sudden cancelling of lessons, frisking of students after the lesson to remove any concealed weapons (pencils) all contributed to the atmosphere of 'high threat - low expectation'. Hopefully our own teaching environments are very different - but can certainly be improved, and perhaps we should remember that, in prison, the classes are usually optional!

Challenge

Visualise in detail a classroom which you use frequently – firstly from your 'teacher perspective', and then from the students' perspective.

SELF-ESTEEM

Imagine you are holding an elegant, fragile, porcelain vase. Feel the weight and shape of it in your hands. Let your fingers run over the smooth cool surface. Sense the delicacy of the fine china. Turn it to admire the intricacy and perfection of the design. Very carefully, rotate this vase so that you can read the markings on the base. Do you see that they spell out your name? Indeed this precious vase is your own - it is your self-esteem.

Sometimes as we go through life we stumble - sometimes indeed a foot is stuck out to trip us - and the vase drops from our hands. It may be chipped, or cracked. It may shatter.

Every student who comes through the classroom door is carrying such a vase. The lucky few may have a vase in pristine condition. Some unfortunates may be carrying little more than a collection of fragments. This damage may show itself in anxiety, or an overcompensation of boisterousness. We may recognise it in the 'fight or flight' response described in the limbic system paragraph on page 72. A student may deliberately switch off and withdraw from participation or become perversely obstructive and irritating to teacher and colleagues.

Part of our teaching job is to ensure that we do what we can to ensure a culture of encouragement where vases are repaired, and certainly not further damaged, by an increased sense of failure and worthlessness. For example, sarcasm is not only the lowest form of wit, it is also the most damaging. It is generally a form of bullying and is a corrupting weed to be searched out, pulled up, and burnt!

It is difficult because we, too, are carrying our own vase – possibly chipped where we have been hurt by unsupportive, negative, student (or colleague) behaviour which seems to attack our credibility. We need support systems to protect ourselves – and strategies for helping students with damaged vases. It's worth noting that a well mended vase may actually be stronger than the unflawed original.

At a basic level we are talking about class management which encourages respect through appropriate correction techniques, thoughtful use of pair and group work – and a constant eye on the 'Tango of Learning'. No pretending – it is very demanding, very fine, work, this – but vital for the enabling of any learning to happen short-term, and also vital for the long-term goal of student autonomy and personal development.

As teachers we have expectations of individual students. These are generally conveyed non-verbally. Do your 'high expectation' students get more eye contact, more challenging tasks - and more help in solving them? Do they get more encouraging nods? And do you re-frame their incorrect answers so that they become acceptable? Are your 'low expectation' students given less time to think about answers, less positive feedback, and non-verbal signals that suggest impatience? If any of this rings a bell, don't feel too guilty - it's only human. However as teachers and therefore by definition 'super-human', we know that we all, and especially when young, tend to believe what significant people say about us (in whatever way the message is conveyed). We will therefore be careful to ensure that the self-fulfilling prophesies we help create for our students are positive ones!

Challenge

Identify and enjoy again three things which have helped your self-esteem this week. (Please do not opt out and say there haven't been any – there have – and they need valuing!)

In **The Road to Daybreak** by Henri Nouwen we meet Janice, Carol, Adam and Rose, all mentally handicapped, and discover the patience and care required to help them pick apples: *"My attitude was to get the apples picked, put them in bags, and go home. But I soon learned that all of that was much less important than to help Rose pick one or two apples, to walk with Janice and Carol looking for apples that hung low enough so that they themselves could reach them...and just sit with Adam in his wheelchair under an apple tree and give him a sense of belonging to the group."*

A survey by Childline showed that a sample of 1,000 secondary school pupils worried more about doing well at school than anything else in their lives. Children as young as twelve were worried about university entrance. Their report concludes:

Examinations involve a judgment delivered publicly, by others, of someone's performance. The fear of being judged is anathema to the sensitive or those with a fragile self-esteem. Parents and tutors should watch out for symptoms which suggest possible psychiatric storms ahead and make every effort to ease the ordeal for the child or undergraduate.

When love and skill work together, expect a masterpiece.
(John Ruskin – brilliant 19c. art critic and philosopher)

Confidence is the supreme gift, the greatest a parent can bestow on their children. *(Susan Greenfield, Professor of Pharmacology, Oxford University)*

Self-esteem is the jet fuel of motivation.
(Murray White)

MULTIPLE INTELLIGENCE THEORY

We start life as 'right-hemisphere' dominant learners - rhythm, songs, bright colours, patterns, intuition provide us with a stream of stimuli. Time goes on, and the input pendulum swings more towards 'left hemisphere' approaches.

Now, it's true to say that linguistic aptitude, and mathematical ability are, and have been, massively important in the development of western civilisation. Gardner's contribution in his book *Frames of Mind* is to discredit the notion that 'intelligence' is primarily or most importantly expressed linguistically and mathematically and can be measured by I.Q. tests, the scores of which then become a way of 'deciding' intelligence, and fixing expectations of future achievement.

It's going to take a while for this recognition and valuing of other forms of intelligence to work its way into the education system in a formal way (if indeed that is what we want to happen). Meanwhile, the awareness is itself a very positive benefit to teachers and learners.

Gardner posits eight 'intelligences'. He claims that these are rooted in biology, particularly that of the brain, and 'seem to reflect the way the nervous system has evolved over the millennia to yield certain discrete kinds of intelligence.' Gardner based his ideas on evidence of different sorts of skills in normal children, research on the way such skills break down under conditions of brain damage, and study of particular groups with remarkable abilities or disabilities. His taxonomy is very useful, although by no means set in tablets of stone. The eight intelligences are:

Musical - a response to music, the ability to play music and derive great satisfaction from it (right hemisphere - but not localised).

Bodily-kinaesthetic - ability to use one's body to express emotion, in dance, for example, or playing sports (motor cortex).

Spatial - the ability to form a mental model of a spatial world, to visualise objects from different angles (right hemisphere).

Logical / mathematical - an ability to reason, calculate, evaluate, but also to construct a solution to a problem non-verbally (left-hemisphere).

Linguistic - a fascination with words and the skill to use language and its structures (left-hemisphere).

Interpersonal - a capacity to recognise and work with distinctions of temperament and moods in others (frontal lobes).

Intrapersonal - access to one's own feelings and to draw on them as a means of understanding and guiding one's behaviour (frontal lobes).

Naturalistic - an affinity with and ability to enjoy and draw strength from the natural world (right-hemisphere, generalised).

Gardner has been criticised for 'missing things out of his list', e.g. there's no 'business intelligence' or 'spiritual intelligence'. Rather more serious is the criticism that, despite an attempt to associate Multiple Intelligence with brain location, his categories still remain 'talents' or 'gifts' or 'aptitudes' rather than identifiable neurological functions.

We must of course ask if there is, in those terms, any such thing as intelligence. Is there anything we do that **isn't** a result of brain activity? Do not traditional IQ tests merely measure the strength of linguistic or reasoning 'aptitudes'? (One definition of **intelligence** is that *'Intelligence is what Intelligence Tests test')*.

STIRRING YOUR INTELLIGENCES

★ **Musical** - Put on a CD which reflects your mood.
★ **Logical/mathematical** - Put four of the classroom activities on page 67 into each intelligence category.
★ **Intrapersonal** - Think how you use your own 'strongest' intelligences in class.
★ **Interpersonal** - Do this activity with someone else. What do you learn about each other?
★ **Bodily-kinaesthetic** - Work out a mime to demonstrate each of these intelligences.
★ **Spatial** - Rearrange the page overleaf to make an effective poster.
★ **Naturalistic** - Identify each of the intelligences with a creature or a landscape.
★ **Linguistic** - Write a rhyming couplet about one of the intelligences.

―――――――――――――――――――――――――――― **Challenge** ―

Look again at the list above. Actually DO the activities!

―――――――――――――――――― **Ponder Point...**

André Gide describes the time when he observed a butterfly being reborn from its chrysalis during a classroom lecture. He was filled with wonder, awe, joy at this metamorphosis, this resurrection. Enthusiastically, he showed it to his professor who replied with a note of disapproval, *"What! Didn't you know that a chrysalis is the envelope of a butterfly? Every butterfly you see has come out of a chrysalis. It's perfectly natural"*. Disillusioned, Gide wrote, *"Yes, indeed, I knew my natural history as well, perhaps better than he . . . But because it was natural, could he not see that it was marvellous? Poor creature! From that day, I took a dislike to him and a loathing to his lessons."*

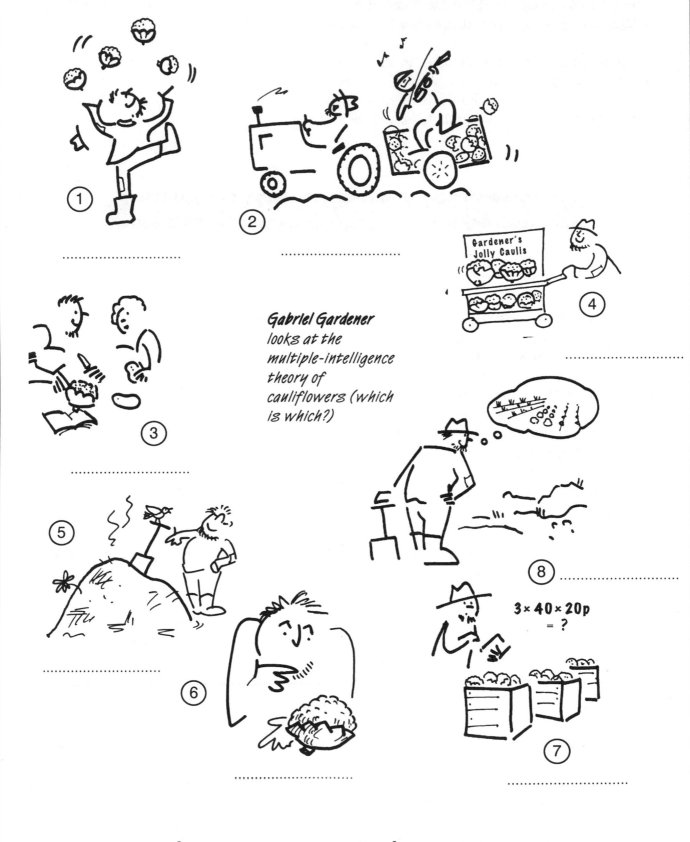

Gabriel Gardener looks at the multiple-intelligence theory of cauliflowers (which is which?)

3 × 40 × 20p = ?

1 Bodily-Kinaesthetic   2 Musical   3 Interpersonal   4 Linguistic
5 Naturalistic   6 Intrapersonal   7 Mathematical   8 Spatial

MULTIPLE INTELLIGENCE CLASSROOM ACTIVITIES

Put each learning/teaching strategy in the appropriate category box ...

a   lectures

b   brainstorming

c   flowers/plants in the room

d   personal goal-setting

e   word puzzles

f   singing

g   working with diagrams

h   peer teaching

i   problem-solving

j   self study

k   fresh air breaks

l   brain gym

m   guided visualisation

n   jazz chants

o   mind maps

p   sequential presentation

q   scenic posters on wall

r   relaxation music

s   rhythm as a memory aid

t   story telling

u   poster layout

v   pair work

w   regular marks/scores for work

x   drama

y   reflective learning activities

z   projects

aa   'classifying' type activities

bb   giving presentations

cc   pelmanism (memory) cards

dd   craft work

ee   choice of background music

ff   keeping a record of work done

Skating

In 'The Prologue', Wordsworth writes about his childhood and, in this passage, describes the excitement of skating on the frozen lakes at night.

Does it, for you, show evidence of all eight 'multiple intelligences'? Do you think Wordsworth was primarily a Visual, Auditory, or Kinaesthetic learner?

And in the frosty season, when the sun
Was set, and visible for many a mile
The cottage windows blazed through twilight gloom,
I heeded not their summons: happy time
It was indeed for all of us - for me
It was a time of rapture! Clear and loud
The village clock tolled six,- I wheeled about,
Proud and exulting like an untired horse
That cares not for his home. All shod with steel,
We hissed along the polished ice in games
Confederate, imitative of the chase
And woodland pleasures,- the resounding horn,
The pack loud chiming, and the hunted hare.
So through the darkness and the cold we flew,
And not a voice was idle; with the din
Smitten, the precipices rang aloud;
The leafless trees and every icy crag
Tinkled like iron; while far distant hills
Into the tumult sent an alien sound
Of melancholy not unnoticed, while the stars
Eastward were sparkling clear, and in the west
The orange sky of evening died away.
Not seldom from the uproar I retired
Into a silent bay, or sportively
Glanced sideway, leaving the tumultuous throng,
To cut across the reflex of a star
That fled, and, flying still before me gleamed
Upon the glassy plain.

Challenge

Think of another poem which has these qualities of movement, introspection, feeling for nature, spatial awareness and so on.

EMOTIONAL INTELLIGENCE

The phenomenal success of Daniel Goleman's best-seller *'Emotional Intelligence'* indicates the depth of fascination with why things go wrong in relationships and why, it seems, irrational surges of emotion can so easily determine behaviour. Clearly there is an overlap here with Gardner's intra and interpersonal intelligences. Like Gardner, Goleman places his book firmly in the context of brain research, and relates his arguments to educational issues.

Teachers have to cope with 'fight or flight' responses of angry or anxious students daily, and any help in understanding and dealing with this is welcome. Goleman gives an account of how the human brain has evolved, and the key role of the limbic system. The amygdala (see page 72) scans incoming signals and reacts to threat by instantly triggering neural crisis signals to the brain which override the normal rational thinking processes of the neo-cortex.

The section 'I'm going to explode' on page 71 is relevant here. Anything that helps us as teachers not to feel the personal target of classroom 'flare up' situations is a useful protection and, likewise, so is an understanding of our own feelings.

Goleman argues that we need to recognise more fully the part emotions play in

every area of behaviour - and also that emotional intelligence can be nurtured and strengthened. Some part of our teaching for success will include teaching empathy, impulse control, and the other fundamentals of emotional competence.

Children can begin to learn from a very early age that other people have different preferences to their own. Acceptance of this is the basis for understanding that, in NLP terms, 'the map is not the territory'. We see a situation in one way, and that's our reality.

Other people may look at the same 'reality' from a different standpoint and have a completely different emotional reaction. Neither party is likely to reach really useful understanding of the territory without at least recognising the valid claim of the other to have their own map - and that neither map is perfect for all circumstances. This is the basis for developing inter and intrapersonal skills, and will be greatly encouraged if children experience adults consistently demonstrating this level of respect.

Ponder Point...

Ambitious civil servants seeking fast track to promotion are encouraged to develop their emotional side and stop macho posturing. The Civil Service office, where senior managers in Government offices are trained, offer courses in emotional intelligence. Emotional Intelligence (EQ) is the ability to monitor one's own and others' feelings and to use those feelings to guide thought and action.

THE JACKAL AND THE GIRAFFE

Rows break out in classrooms - and staffrooms. People feel threatened, and become frustrated by the seemingly incomprehensible behaviour of others. How can we head off destructive flare-ups - or at least limit the damage?

The most effective tools are often very simple. Marshall Rosenberg, an authority on keeping discussions focused between two parties - both at a personal and an inter-government level, may help here. Marshall Rosenberg's work on **non-violent communication** contains the idea of the Jackal and the Giraffe. Let me explain their significance and power.

Marshall works with groups of people who are in conflict. He helps them become aware that the language they use may be a significant factor in the conflict. I quote: *"For teaching purposes I refer to the language of blame and condemnation as 'Jackal language' because when we are on the receiving end of it we feel as if we are about to be eaten by a jackal. On the other hand, I have observed that people who respond compassionately to themselves and others speak a language which connects them to the life within themselves and others. I refer to this as Giraffe language (because it is the language of the heart and giraffes have the largest heart of any land animal; they live their lives with gentleness and strength). Giraffe language allows us to assert our values and at the same time to support others and realise their values."*

This simple contrast (Marshall uses two glove puppets) helps us to hear what we are saying to other people in situations of tension. Suddenly we realise how fluent we are in 'Jackal' - for most people it's a mother tongue. Under pressure we resort to sarcasm, name-calling, 'put-downs': tactics which isolate and judge others. When we speak 'Giraffe' we engage in a dialogue to talk about what is going on in ourselves - not what is wrong with others. The 'dance of Giraffe', as Marshall puts it, involves expressing our own feelings without criticising others and requesting, rather than demanding, what we would like to be done.

Just listening to yourself with other people's 'ears' will quickly identify Jackal language. It's an image which is very recognisable and is well worth sharing with anyone with whom you have a relationship – professional or domestic!

Have a look at **Non-violent communication-A language of compassion,**   Marshall Rosenberg, Puddledance Press 1999

Challenge

Watch a TV discussion progamme tonight. Note examples of 'giraffe' and of 'jackal' and observe the effect that each has.

I'M GOING TO EXPLODE !*!

Very few teachers say they have not at times been driven to, or over, the brink. People develop their own ways of coping with the red mist in front of the eyes. Here are some...

Instant

★ Breathe slowly and count to ten.
★ Remind yourself that you are the teacher, an adult, and should set a good example in how to behave.
★ Think about what's on the tip of your tongue to say. How would you feel if someone said it to you?

Short-term

★ Go outside for a breath of fresh air. Chew something (not your nails or lower lip).
★ Shout if you need to!
★ If possible, grab a moment on your own and think about why you are angry. Is it really because of what's happening in class or is something else upsetting you?
★ Visualise a beautiful tranquil scene. This can help to calm you down.
★ Share the problem with a colleague. There's emotional and practical support in not feeling isolated.
★ Humour is sometimes the best remedy. Try to see the funny side if you can.

Slightly longer short-term

★ Plan some treats for yourself to provide a lift of spirits.

Medium-term

Occasional outbursts are normal, but if you are living in a pattern of stress which drives you to rage you need to recognise the damage this could be doing you. Take stock, don't be proud, and look seriously for support.

This advice has been very loosely adapted from a leaflet produced by the National Society for the Prevention of Cruelty to Children.

Ponder Point...

I discovered that I always have choices – and sometimes it's only a choice of attitude.   *Judith Knowlton*

THE 'FIGHT OR FLIGHT' RESPONSE?

The brain receives signals from the outside world and also from the body. For the most part the brain responds to the internal signals of its own accord - taking care of things like breathing, heartbeat and blood pressure. The system by which it does this is known as the **autonomic nervous system**.

This system operates in two modes. Most of the time it functions in its 'peace' mode - the heart beat is slow and steady, food is being steadily digested. Under threat however, such as a sudden stressful situation, it switches to a 'war' footing - the ancient primitive condition of an emergency response to ensure survival.

In this situation the **amygdala**, an almond-shaped cluster of structures forming part of the limbic system, hijacks control from the neo-cortex and orders the brain stem to fix the face in an expression of aggression or terror. Heartbeat and blood pressure go up to pump oxygen to the vital organs via the blood. Adrenaline is released to power up the nervous system for aggression or for running away. Blood flows to the hands to make it easier to wield weapons, the blood runs cold - or feels as if it does - because it's drained from the face and channelled to the leg muscles. (Is this why we 'kick out' at things when we are angry?) Everything that the brain normally does, thinking things out rationally for example, gets switched off in the face of this 'need-to-survive reaction' and we lose our self-control....

In a classroom situation we recognise the effects in displays of aggressive or disruptive behaviour, and also in the body-language of students who are 'defending themselves' by not participating in the lesson or not relating to those around them.

There is no way of kidding such people that everything is alright when their autonomic nervous system is sending a quite different and very powerful message through the brain to the body. Strategies to achieve a 'Tango of Learning' situation are necessary. See page 60.

— **Challenge**

Recognise a situation where this reaction has occurred inappropriately and do something about limiting the damage from it.

A linguistic intelligence joke.

Q.: What did the articulate drunk say to his doctor?
A: I'd rather have a bottle in front of me than a frontal lobotomy.

INTRAPERSONAL AND INTERPERSONAL TEAM BUILDING
Two 'Affective' activities

My shield

I like this activity because it allows people to say as much or as little as they wish about what 'makes them tick'.

Allow some minutes to think about the categories and draw a picture in each segment. Drawing the pictures is important. Artistic quality doesn't matter. The pictures stir imagination and memory.

The shields are only for one-to-one private conversation. Participants take turns to talk their partner through the pictures, to explain them and say why they have made this choice.

Because of the self-investment in the exercise people give and receive very positive esteem from their partner and often make contact at a less superficial level than usual. Trust and confidence is enhanced.

If you would like to see _my_ shield it is on page 105 - but I'd rather tell you about it (and see and hear about yours) than have you read the text.

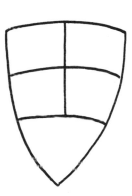

The Blobbies at sea!

We are all part of numerous organisations - work, family, clubs and so on. It's unlikely that we always feel absolutely happy with our position in all these networks.

The blobbies provide a protected opportunity to articulate feelings about our current role as **we** see it, how we think **others** see us, and what _change_ in role we would like to have.

The 'match the adjectives to the figure' activity generates discussion of feelings, and even this may be useful in building a positive learning community.

MY SHIELD

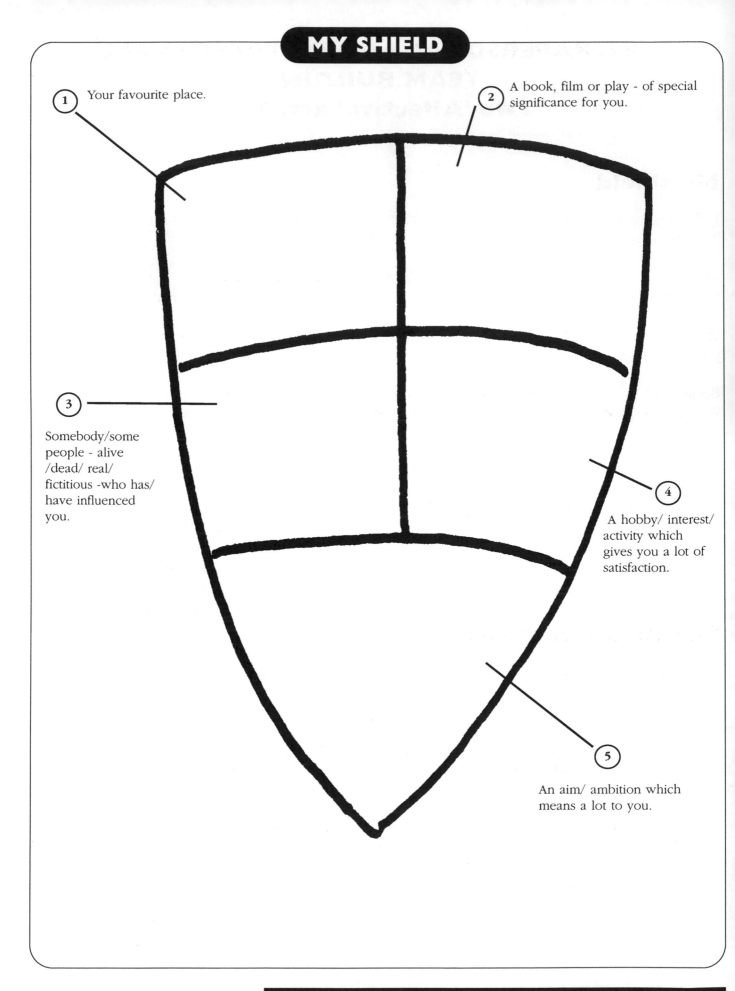

1. Your favourite place.

2. A book, film or play - of special significance for you.

3. Somebody/some people - alive /dead/ real/ fictitious -who has/ have influenced you.

4. A hobby/ interest/ activity which gives you a lot of satisfaction.

5. An aim/ ambition which means a lot to you.

BLOBBIES AT SEA . . .

1 Match the adjectives below to the figures in the picture. See if your colleagues agree which Blobby is which.

2 Choose an organisation which you belong to - you don't have to identify it to anyone else - and decide which Blobby you are at the moment.

3 Think. Is this actually how **others** see you?

4 Which Blobby you would *like* to be - and think about how to effect the change!

farsighted
anxious
left out
individualist
supportive
practical
team person
creative
threatened
destructive
reliable
foolish
bored
enthusiastic
needing encouragement
obstructionist
hardworking
figurehead
in control
desperate

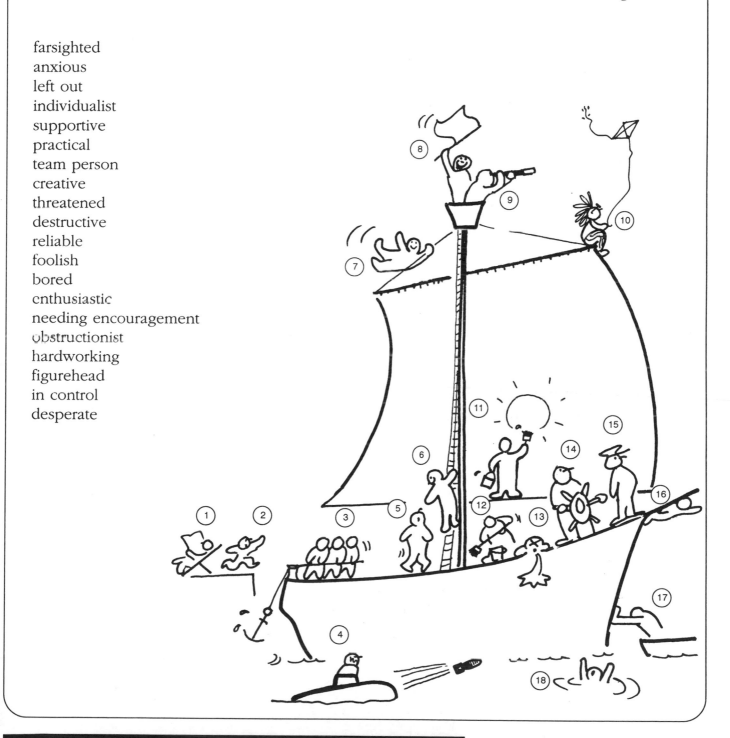

STIRRING THE MEMORY TRACES

★ If **2** is the Right Hemisphere and **4** the limbic system, what are **3** and **5**?   Page 16

★ Draw one of the things from **my** Treasure Chest - and **one** from **yours**.   Page 34

★ If the **cat** is in **love** with the **bird**, what is the **book** about? - and what does the **spaceman** have?   Page 49

★ Which **Blobby** are you?   Page 77

★ **S** is for.........   and.........   and.........?   Page 62

★ Recall (and enjoy again) the five picture symbols you drew on your **shield**.   Page 76

★ Which is **your** dominant learning style?
Have you done anything today that supports your opinion?   Page 40

★ Identify (from the students you teach) a strongly **kinaesthetic** learner.   Page 41

★ What do these symbols represent?
Draw 3 others in the sequence.   Page 46

★ Which is the Odd One Out?
Gardner, Lozanov, Glia, Feuerstein   Pages 56

AND PLANTING SOME NEW ONES

(or whetting your appetite)

THE SUGGESTOPEDIC ELEPHANT

"Suggestopedia works in harmony with people logically, emotionally and ethically."

As we have seen, Suggestopedia is the key inspiration which draws together and provides a rationale for so much which clearly works and makes sense.

Lozanov's work has been the 'engine' for so may 'learning' societies around the world. See it as a gold mine. Not everything that comes out will be of top value to you. Some nuggets you will regard as worthless. You will find pure gold in other locations than this mine - but Suggestopedia is a very rich, deep, and only partially-explored mine. It is certainly not yet a fully-exploited mine.

This, and Dr. Lozanov's teaching, have inspired the Suggestopedic elephant story which follows - written in dramatised form and in short lines that the eye takes in.

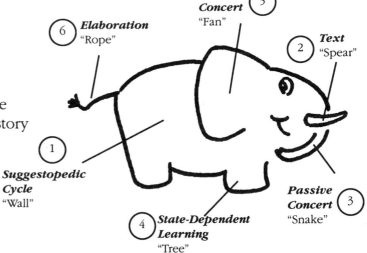

In my own teaching I don't follow Lozanov's teaching cycle exactly, and probably you won't either, but it's worth knowing a bit more about this major contribution to the BRAIN-*friendly* revolution. Have a look at page 57 before reading the J.G.Saxe poem opposite, which expresses so entertainingly how easy it is to jump to conclusions, and also that the whole is generally much greater than the sum of the parts!

The Blind Men and the Elephant

It was six men of Hindostan
To learning much inclined,
Who went to see the elephant
(Though all of them were blind),
That each by observation
Might satisfy his mind.

The first approached the elephant,
And happening to fall
Against its broad and sturdy *side*,
At once began to bawl,
'God bless me! but the elephant
Is very like a wall!'

The second, feeling of the *tusk*,
Cried, 'Ho! what have we here
So very round and smooth and sharp?
To me 'tis mighty clear
This wonder of an elephant
is very like a spear!'

The third approached the animal,
And happening to take
The squirming *trunk* within his hands,
Thus boldly up and spake;
'I see,' quoth he, 'the elephant
Is very like a snake!'

The fourth reached out his eager hand
And felt about the *knee*;
'What most this mighty beast is like
Is mighty plain,' quoth he;
''Tis clear enough the elephant
Is very like a tree!'

The fifth who chanced to touch the *ear*
Said, 'E'en the blindest man
Can tell what this resembles most;
Deny the fact who can,
This marvel of an elephant
Is very like a fan!'

The sixth no sooner had begun
About the beast to grope
Than, seizing on the swinging *tail*
That fell within his scope,
'I see,' quoth he, 'the elephant
Is very like a rope!'

And so these men of Hindostan
Disputed loud and long,
Each in his own opinion
Exceeding stiff and strong,
Though each was *partly* in the right,
They all were in the wrong.

J. G. Saxe

THE SUGGESTOPEDIC ELEPHANT!

Narrator   Like the six blind men of Hindostan,
we'll feel our way around each part.
Discuss the methods, stages, art, then see if we can
sense the heart of **our** particular 'elephant'.

Explorer 1   First, the elephant's 'side' or 'wall'. I'll tell you how
clinical *research* evolved into a *teaching method*.
The three phases of the **SUGGESTOPEDIC CYCLE**
develop from Lozanov's psychotherapy work.
First, **create** confidence.
10   Next, **change** the things that limit growth and
then, **consolidate** results.
The adaptation for teaching follows broadly similar
lines.
The **INTRODUCTION** creates a suitable learning
environment.
This light-hearted planting of *memory traces*
presents target material in a *global way* with
drama, humour, visuals.
Then comes the **SESSION** - actually two phases.
The Active Concert read to classical music
20   heightens *learning expectation* and presents the
whole body of lesson material.
The Passive Concert follows on.
Listening to Baroque music the body is *relaxed,*
the brain is alert, receiving information without
conscious effort.
The **ELABORATION** stage *activate*s material, recycling
it through games, songs, role play, repetition.
This is the fine work of fixing deeper - moving
from twilight recognition to the clearly accessible.
In Suggestopedia everything is *structured*
30   *linguistically, psychologically.*
This cycle must surely be the essential basis of the
method?

Explorer 2 Thank you. Thank you. I come next and feel the 'elephant's tusk' of TEXT.

A Suggestopedic text has special features, most obviously, a *dramatic form*.

Organised in *Acts*, with *storyline* and *all-star cast*, and text arranged in *chunks* the eye assimilates.

Themes should *build-up*, not depress, and never threaten emotionally.

As learners create a *role identity* a world of imagination opens up.

For language learners, *translation* into mother tongue placed side by side with target text provides *security*. Most subjects can be prepared this way.

The *lengthy text* is quite deliberate and overcomes suggestive norms which limit expectations.

The rich, enticing, central text contains the *learning content*.

Other things crop up, of course, but the text material is elaborated, reworked by repetition, games and sketches.

Formidable, elegant, and admired, the text is a glory of Suggestopedia.

Explorer 3 A 'trunk' call's third, and you've just heard of special texts and three phase cycles.

These are important - but I guess you don't learn much when under stress! To tap *reserve powers of learning* we need a *mental state of calm*.

You'll know how, in an alpha state learning is faster because information by-passes logical processing.

Let me explain the importance of the PSEUDO-PASSIVE CONCERT.

Baroque music is harmonious with notes in simple but related steps.

Then it's ornamented, parts are added, carefully constructed - pleasant, not too rich.

Such music *adjusts and balances* the listener's psychological and body state.

Outwardly relaxed, inwardly calm, receptive. *Mental energy* is directed to the learning task.

To control the relaxation level learners sit comfortably in normal chairs, the text is read at normal speed without distortion - and to faster Baroque movements.

Thus avoiding any chance of falling into pre-lunch trance! You may agree this strategy developed from understandings in neurology gives Suggestopedia uniqueness, and its power.

40

50

60

70

80

Explorer 4 And here's a fourth explorer - me! I'll grasp the beast about the 'knee'.

Suggestopedia is **STATE DEPENDENT LEARNING.**

90 How you feel is fundamental to success.

That's more than 'wanting to do well', or 'trying hard'.

Psychological and physical conditions should be right.

Teacher authority is the main factor in the learning set-up of motivation and feelings.

Learners need to be *in harmony* with teacher, subject, colleagues - and themselves.

If not, barriers will operate.

The Critical-Logical rejects whatever appears not sensible.

100 The Intuitive-Affective rejects whatever harms emotionally.

The Ethical rejects conflicting systems of belief.

That's quite a task! I hear you ask, 'How does a teacher harmonize all that?' Essentially, by building *confidence* and *trust*.

A suggestopedic teacher, highly skilled in his or her own subject, is also aware of what Lozanov calls *'Double planeness'*.

Tone of voice, body language, fine pictures on the wall, the *stream of stimuli* received unconsciously that's so important in communicating meaning.

110 The teacher's authority is not a form of bullying but comes from readiness to share knowledge and showing to learners that they, and the subject, are of real value.

Explorer 5 Please listen now to a music fan.

Discussions on Suggestopedia focus more on reading to music than on any other component.

You've heard about the Passive Concert.

It's now time for me to give some information on - the **ACTIVE.**

Voice quality is so important.

120 The teacher *follows the music closely*, moving between the *voice positions* high, medium, low.

The teacher stands and reads with *dignity* giving emphasis by pauses, allowing phrases to echo in the memory.

It's an *artistic performance* and should be treated as a highlight.

This reading creates brain expectation of important news.

130 The music's rich contrasts of moods activate the brain's *right hemisphere*.

Learners actively follow the text creating memory traces and associations.

The weight and solemnity of the Session powerfully suggest that new material will be assimilated and automated without strain or fatigue as the concert gives enriching language and aesthetic pleasure.

Explorer 6 The elephant's tale is not yet ended.

140 Number six provides the fix! How is it that children learn so fast? Must we put off our adulthood for games and make-believe?
Well, these things have a part to play.
But, first things first.
The *fun* comes from the *joy of learning*.
All the *rich variety* of songs, rhymes, puzzles, dance, serve to enhance the understanding that we're not a box of intellect, but also learn through bodily response and feelings.

150 The brain function of the hypothalamus and limbic systems play a full part in forming what we are.

Learning subconsciously as well as consciously, we develop our whole *personality*.
As attention is focused on a game, information is internalised rapidly, without an intellectual filter.
So too Peripherals convey their teaching point 'unnoticed'.
Props for acting banish nervousness through laughter.
Adopting new names, creating new identities, suggestopedically gives a freedom to move, feel, and enjoy a *growing creativity*.
But remember, the bit that comes last, this

160 ELABORATION, the 'elephant's tail' is actually *highly organised* connecting and reviewing the whole text by doing things, sharing feelings, having fun.

Narrator So. We've heard from six explorers who praised 'side', 'tusk' and 'trunk', and rightly honoured 'knee', and 'ear', and 'tail'.
A splendid creature - our Suggestopedic elephant.
Before you climb on for a ride

170 Here's something to think about and decide.
We clearly see the value of each part.....
What do **you** think is the elephant's 'heart'?

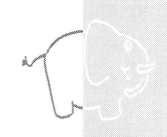

"There must be great love for one's profession - and for one's fellow man."
- Dr. Lozanov

Decoding and Elaborations

1. There were six explorers. Choose a colour for each, read the text again and use 6 different coloured pens to <u>underline</u> all the phrases in *italics* or in **bold**.
   Are you sure what each phrase means?
   You might want to look at the Glossary opposite.

2. Can you find a phrase from the text which goes with each of these pictures?
   Connect them to the pictures.

Example

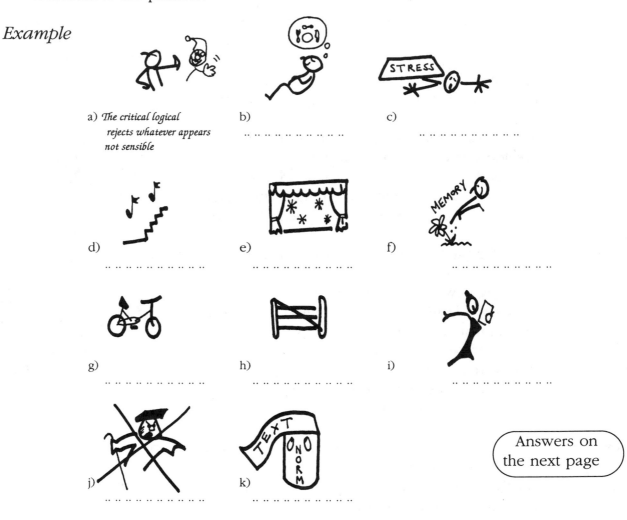

a) *The critical logical rejects whatever appears not sensible*

b) .. ..

c) .. ..

d) .. ..

e) .. ..

f) .. ..

g) .. ..

h) .. ..

i) .. ..

j) .. ..

k) .. ..

Answers on the next page

3. What in suggestopedic terms, do these parts of the elephant represent: Ear? Side? Tusk?

Challenge

How about trying a dramatised recital of 'The Blind Men and the Elephant'? with some Active and then Passive Concert reading music?

GLOSSARY OF TERMS

Suggestopedia (Suggestopaedia) is a method. It is most often used in language training but is also applied to many other types of training. Suggestopedy is the science behind it. Dr. Lozanov now favours the term 'Desuggestive Learning'.

The Session	Lozanov's term for the Active and Passive concert phases of the Suggestopedic cycle.
Introduction	The subject matter is presented in a lively way using pictures, props, acting, and involving the students.
Active Concert	The teacher reads the text aloud to music - the voice modulating to follow lively classical music.
Pseudo Passive Concert	The learner is asked to relax, and appears to be very relaxed and 'passive' but the brain is still active at a different level to usual. The teacher reads aloud with clear pronunciation, natural intonation, and at normal speed to soft Baroque music.
Elaboration	Activities which practise the target material. Time-wise, the major part of the cycle.
Text in chunks	Text divided into shortish lines and blocks.
Suggestive norms	What people expect/are expected to be able to learn in a given time.
Alpha state	A term for when the body is calm and the activity of the brain slows to about 7-12 cycles per second.
State dependency	How well you learn depends on how you feel about the subject, yourself, the teacher, where you are etc. Your 'state of mind'.
Barrier	Whatever interferes with a positive attitude to learning. Lozanov lists three main categories, as in our text.
Voice positions	Try speaking with a 'head' voice, a 'throat' voice and a 'stomach' voice.
Right and Left	The Right hemisphere of the brain responds to music, art and spatial relationships while the Left processes analytically. This is a useful - although simplified - metaphor.
Double Planeness	Everything from the teacher's body language to how the room is arranged sends the same message – that of giving value to what is happening.
Peripherals	Pictures/posters/objects with learning content. Normally not the focus of attention, but noticed sub-consciously.
Hypothalmus & limbic system	Very complex areas of the brain associated with memory and emotion.
Decoding	A stage (usually between Active and Passive Concerts) of making sure the text is understood. Translation may be used or student-student, student-teacher discussion/questioning.

Answers (from page 86)

a) line 97; b) 82, c) 62, d) 70, e) 38, f) 15, g) 31, h)96, i)127, j) 109, k) 50

87

Mind Map Review

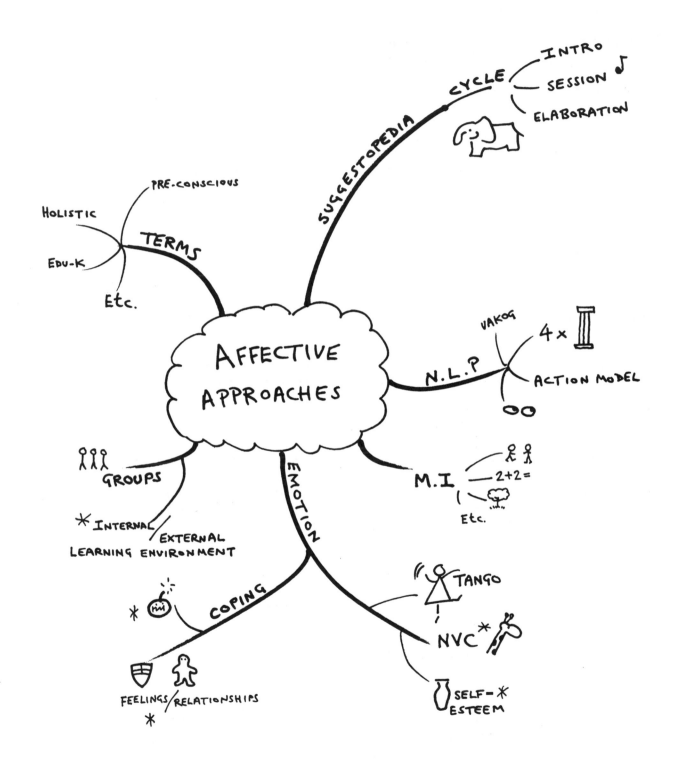

ONE PICTURE IS WORTH . . .

Applications

Cover story

By this stage of the book you will certainly have picked it up and put it down several times, and probably noticed a new element of the cover design each time you did so. The cover, like memory, is multi-layered, capable of changing significance through experience, and capable of eliciting a different response from each individual. In case you haven't yet had a close look, here are a few things to check for:

- symbols of multiple intelligences....
- Front: naturalistic, linguistic, spatial, intrapersonal, musical, logical-mathematical,
- - and on the back - kinaesthetic and interpersonal

Have you found a few places that have significance in the development and dissemination of ideas such as Alexandria, Gettysburg, the Italy of the Renaissance, Shakespeare's plays?

You'll have noticed the cog of precision engineering, - and the brain, of course, but have you spotted the two brain-friendly symbols, the pointing finger (left or right handed?), some brain activity - and a reference to the suggestopedic elephant?

Allow scope to your own intuition.

How do you interpret, for example, the white birds? And the formless areas of colour? The choice of colour? The vertical ribbons of letters, or of reflected light, front top right and on the back cover?

Mind map

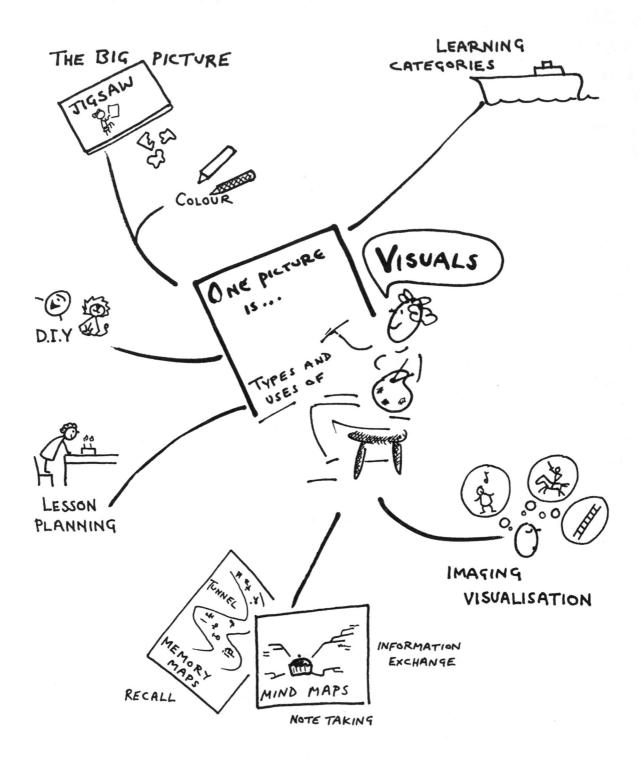

THE BIG PICTURE

Think of a jigsaw puzzle which someone has tipped out on to the kitchen table. Something inside you says *"I'll just fit a few pieces together"*. It's a hard thing to pass by without that response isn't it? The left hemisphere of the brain starts to sort out bits with straight edges, and eventually finds two that fit together... and then another...and so on. The right hemisphere is saying *" I want to see the picture on the box! If I can see the picture I'll know what I'm supposed to be making, and I'll have an idea where all the blue bits go."*

It's convenient to design text books on the very structured test-as-you-go, step-by-step approach. There's nothing wrong with that as long as the right hemisphere also gets a chance, and can glimpse *'the picture on the box'*.

Language courses traditionally move in a carefully structured progression through different tenses (although we certainly didn't learn our mother tongue in that way), so here is *Paula the painter* to give a slightly bigger picture of English grammar. First, imagine yourself in Paula's studio with bright colours all around, and that instantly recognisable smell of oil paint...

> ## Challenge
> In what areas of my subject could my students benefit by seeing more of the 'big picture'?

with her Pictures of English Tenses

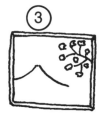

How quickly can you connect these sentences to the pictures?

a   I've painted hundreds of pictures
b   While I was painting this picture it started to rain
c   I'm painting my cat at the moment
d   This was painted by Leonardo in 1503
e   I paint landscapes and animal pictures
f   Tomorrow I'm going to paint my dog
g   Last year I painted Mount Fuji in Japan

Mark Fletcher

USE OF COLOUR

Colour coding information is very Brain-friendly in that it is logical, systematic, visually appealing and also involves the learner in doing something. It provides a spring-board for the brain to build up patterns of connections.

Here's an example from the Pictures of English Tenses overview on the previous page.

Take a set of felt tip pens.

Dark Blue is our colour for things we usually do, everyday actions, so underline *'I paint landscapes and animal pictures'* in **Dark Blue** and write that sentence by picture 1.

Light Blue is the colour for things happening at the moment so underline *'I'm painting my cat'* in **Light Blue**.

Similarly for *'I painted'* (**Dark Brown**) and *'I was painting'* (**Light Brown**).

Take a green peppermint sweet. Suck it. Swallow it. You've eaten the sweet. The sweet has gone - but you can still taste the peppermint. (This is for our gustatory learners!) Peppermint green is our colour for the **Present Perfect** *'I've painted hundreds of pictures...'*

And all **Futures** are a bright, sunny **yellow**.

You might prefer different colour associations, but the point is that the Right Hemisphere is getting a chance to be involved through **colour and visuals** (and, of course, we can also act out the Paula scenario). It has provided the students with another, additional route, to understanding. The teacher also has a non-intrusive method of correction. If you hear *'I have seen a good film last night'* just indicating the brown felt tip is enough of a memory prompt for the student to self-correct to *'I saw ...'*.

In language classes I find that colour coding appeals to young learners, but also, interestingly, that it provides a real lifeline for many older learners who have a 'block' about grammar explanations. It enables them to construct non-verbal understanding of how the Tense system works from their own associations. This, in turn, provides a great boost to confidence.

Challenge

Regardless of the subject, can I systematically use colour coding to help my more 'Right Brain' students?

USING PICTURES FOR LEARNING CATEGORIES

Sorting things into categories is a good way of encoding learning material. See page 44. It involves matching like with like by making associations, sometimes using a previous knowledge and sometimes in a right hemisphere intuitive way. It also often means reaching solutions via the logical left hemisphere process of elimination. The process is made more interesting (and hence more **effective**) by providing simple 'visual boxes'.

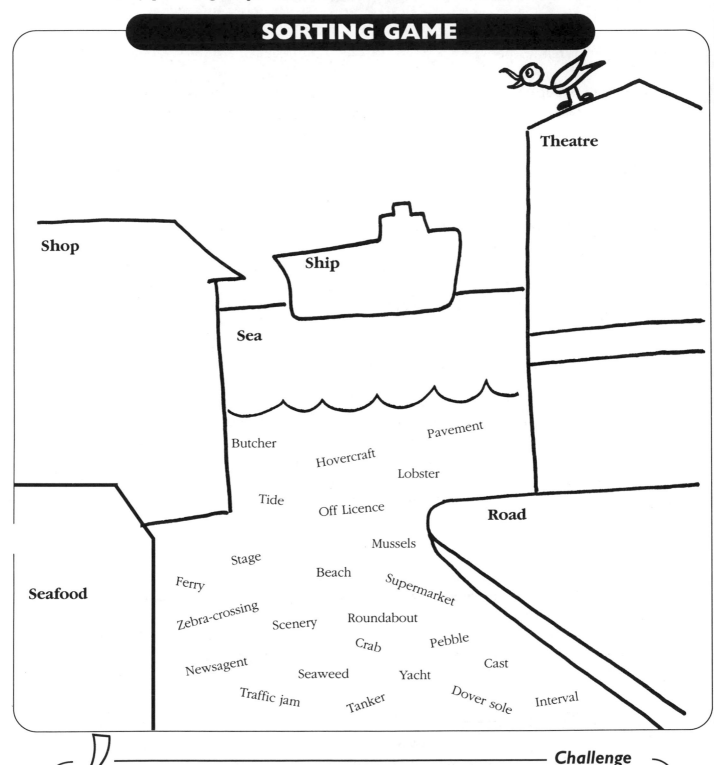

SORTING GAME

Theatre

Shop

Ship

Sea

Seafood

Road

Butcher
Pavement
Hovercraft
Lobster
Tide
Off Licence
Mussels
Stage
Beach
Supermarket
Ferry
Zebra-crossing
Scenery
Roundabout
Crab
Pebble
Newsagent
Cast
Seaweed
Yacht
Traffic jam
Tanker
Dover sole
Interval

Challenge

If you haven't already done so, take five different coloured felt tips and colour code the categories. Instantly you will recognise a new element of brain stimulation.

Making the exercise more communicative

Interaction adds another 'layer' of self-investment and meaning to the memorising process. Let's apply this principle to the activity opposite.

Instructions

i) **Add** one more word to each category,

ii) **See** what words your near **neighbours** have added.

iii) Look again at the category boxes. **Choose** any three words or items that are new or interesting and **write** them on the back of the page. These are your 'star' words.

iv) You have two minutes to **move** around the room to **find** one person who has chosen the same three words - and one person whose choice is completely different.

v) **Look** at your own 'star' words again. **Invent and write** a short story or paragraph which contains those three words.

vi) Find a partner and **tell** each other your stories. The **listener's** job is to **identify** the 'star' words you have used.

Challenge

Think of several information categories in your own teaching subject, and, in the space below, design a similar activity to the one opposite with appropriate visual boxes and words/items.

PICTURES IN THE MIND

Imaging – Guided Visualisation

Computers and television provide wonderful access to images, mainly – but by no means entirely – visual. They also offer great opportunities to develop imaginative lay-out and presentation skills. They are an enormously useful teaching and learning asset. One small word of caution may not be out of place, however. Virtual reality is becoming more and more a fact of life, and the silicon revolution gives us instant and intriguing standard images. Are we therefore at risk of undervaluing and eventually diminishing the extraordinary facility of our own brains to create worlds from the sound of a voice or a fragment of description? Our imagination links memories and feelings into pictures that are completely original and unique, and with which our limbic systems create a sense of identity and ownership.

Many learners find that sitting quietly and allowing pictures to form in the mind is a welcome and refreshing change of pace from the business and busyness of the day. I frequently use a variation of this at the end of an intensive lesson. We sit quietly, relax (see page 118) put on some gentle music while I 'talk through' the key points again. This ties in well with the points on recycling and 'passive learning' made in our section on 'from short to long-term memory' page 43.

Guided visualisation involves creating pictures in your mind whilst following a script. Although the form of the 'journey' is controlled by the script, the content remains unpredictable. We know that an experience with a powerful attachment to emotion is more likely to be retained in the long-term memory. By inviting learners to attune to their feelings during visualisation, we can ensure this has a better chance of taking place. The following pages give some simple ways to recognise and usefully release some of this creative imagination, in class, through visualisation. There's nothing new in this, of course. Writers do it all the time. Here's an example from Shakespeare himself to lend authority to the case.....
Sit back. You are in the Globe theatre and the 'Chorus' walks on to the stage....

Can this cockpit hold
The vasty fields of France? or may we cram
Within this wooden O the very casques
That did affright the air at Agincourt?
O, pardon! Since a crooked figure may attest
in little place a million;
And let us, cyphers in this great accompt,
On your imaginary forces work.

Suppose within the girdle of these walls
Are now confin'd two mighty monarchies,
Whose high upreared and abutting fronts
The perilous narrow ocean parts asunder:
Piece out our imperfections with your thoughts:
Into a thousand parts divide one man,
And make imaginary puissance;
Think, when we talk of horses that you see them
Printing their proud hoofs i' the receiving earth;
For 'tis your thoughts that now must deck our kings,
Carry them here and there; jumping o'er times,
Turning the accomplishment of many years
Into an hour-glass:
(Prologue to HenryV)

VISUALISATION LADDER

Quite often teachers (or rather, the students) are faced with using comprehension-type texts or factual but bland accounts of processes. A few moments to form an image provides the student with a right hemisphere, limbic system 'investment' in the materials. The imagination is engaged so motivation is greater.

Before you read the newspaper article 'Carlo the Chocolate maker' over the page, here is an adaptable visualisation ladder – a series of simple, open-ended prompts to help the listener or reader form a picture in their mind.

(Allow a short pause - about 5 seconds - after each prompt.)

First, imagine the taste and texture of your favourite chocolates!

We're going to read (listen to) an article about Carlo Melchior.

Carlo is a chocolate maker who came to England fourteen years ago.

See him in your imagination.

Is he a tall man? Or is he of medium height? Or short?

Is he slim? Or heavily built?

How would you describe his face?

What sort of hair does he have?

Does he have a beard or moustache? Or is he clean-shaven?

Think about his personality...what's he like as a person?

He has an interesting hobby. What is it?

He's married to Linda, and they run the business together.

How long have they been married?

Do they both like the same music? The same holidays?

Carlo is looking very happy today. Why?

Focus the picture of Carlo on a screen in your mind's eye.

And now describe him to your neighbour. Are your chocolate makers similar or very different?

Some advice. As a student, I get annoyed if I follow the prompts, create a character, then turn to the article and find I'm 'wrong' because my mental picture conflicts with factual information in the text. When you encourage students to create their own personally valid picture take care to avoid such a frustration. It works against the intended positive motivation.

Challenge

Work out a visualisation ladder – a person, a place, a context, which is relevant to a lesson you will teach next week.

CARLO THE CHOCOLATE MAKER

Melchior Chocolates started as a challenge. Two years ago, Carlo Melchior was making chocolates as a hobby. He and his wife Linda decided that, if they could sell their chocolates to the best food shop in the country, they would go into business.

The Melchiors travelled from Devon, rather naively they admit, with samples, children, and pushchairs to see the buyer of an exclusive London food store and won their first order - for ten kilos of hand-made chocolates.

Not wishing to risk that precious initial order in the post, they delivered it to the store themselves, wiping out their profit margin in train fares. However, it was the first step in turning Carlo's hobby into a flourishing business. Chocolate, explains Linda, is an important part of Swiss life.

When her husband, Carlo, came to England 14 years ago he could not find high-quality chocolates, so he returned to Switzerland to learn how to make them himself. For ten years, while he and Linda ran a restaurant, he produced chocolates for an appreciative circle of diners, family and friends. The Melchiors sold their restaurant business four years ago and took a year off to renovate an old brewery. Carlo continued to make chocolates for fun. But that first large order persuaded the Melchoirs that there was business potential. Start-up costs for the business were about £100,000, but it is difficult, says Linda, to be precise. Within two months of starting up, they needed help to cope with the volume of orders and found a plentiful supply of local labour. No elaborate equipment or machines are used to produce the range of 40 truffles and pralines and Carlo is constantly testing and introducing new lines.

Carlo works with expensive raw ingredients - fresh Devon cream and Swiss chocolate, which is high in cocoa fats. The taste is superior to British chocolates, which are made from vegetable fat to reduce the price. The Melchiors know every detail of the chocolate they use, from the meadows in the Alps where the cows are pastured to the little Swiss factory which makes the chocolate.

Melchior chocolates are packed in hand-made boxes made by a small company in Worcestershire. The boxes are strong enough to be sent through the post.

The Melchiors can produce a ton of chocolates a week at peak times and their Christmas turnover has trebled in a year. Carlo says they have no ambitions to compete with the big manufacturers. *"We want to stay a small, personal business with a very high-quality product,"* he explains, *"making something which people really enjoy."*

MIND MAPS

Mind mapping is a way of taking information and keeping it open, available and adaptable. Its value is that it operates very flexibly, seeking and creating patterns in a similar way to the brain. A mind map makes connections between ideas in a variety of ways as they occur, and is not tied to a linear progression or a fixed time sequence.

In a simple way, you start with a main topic in the centre of the page and lead branches from it by noting relevant words as new lines of thought occur. Almost certainly ideas will cross-reference, and this can be shown by colour coding or a symbol. In fact, the more visual and colourful the mind map, the more individual and interesting it will appear, and the easier it will be to revive the associations when it is reviewed at a later date.

Mind map – Carlo the chocolate maker

Read the article on the previous page very quickly, and add information to the mind map below.

(A mind map means a lot to the person who has drawn it and, generally, not much to anyone else. Your version will not look much like mine – and that is how it should be!)

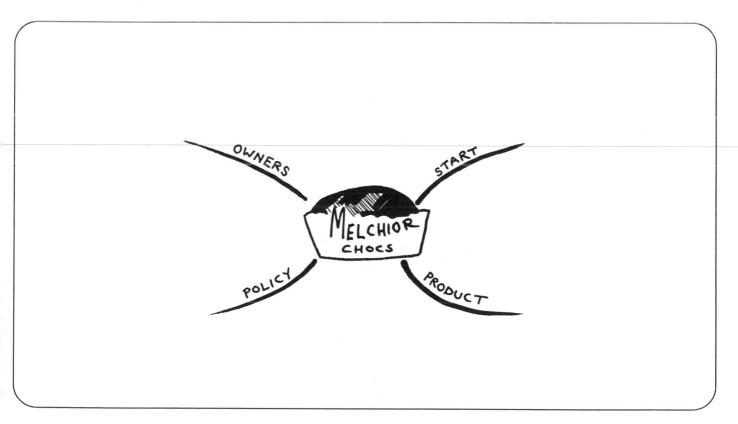

MAKING THE TEXT MORE COMMUNICATIVE

As we have seen, there's a 'brain' advantage in turning 'reading' exercises into something more communicative, perhaps an interview. This is easy to do. Two suggestions:

Suggestion A.

- Half the class are reporters. Before interviewing Carlo they use the mind map as the basis for writing out six or so questions. While they do that, the other students (Carlo) rapidly read the *Chocolate Maker* to get information. In pairs, each 'Reporter' then interviews 'Carlo' and jots down information on their mind maps.

- Improve on this by adding an element of role-play. (Tour of the chocolate factory. Free samples!)

- Make sure that the 'Interview' role-play involves the reporter arriving - a welcome - a farewell (not just Question/Answer/Finish).

- Involve 'Linda' as well so that the reporter is getting information from two people and there is more interaction.

Suggestion B.

Set up the activity so that students

1 Copy the mind map
2 Put the mind map aside
3 Skim-read the article
4 Put the article aside and take up the mind map
5 Jot down notes on their mind map
6 Compare information with their partner - add/correct/note "missing items"
   (A huge amount of 'turning over' of information has gone on up to now and has created a hunger to check on disputed or missing bits.)
7 Go back to the article and complete the mind map. It will now look *something* like this:

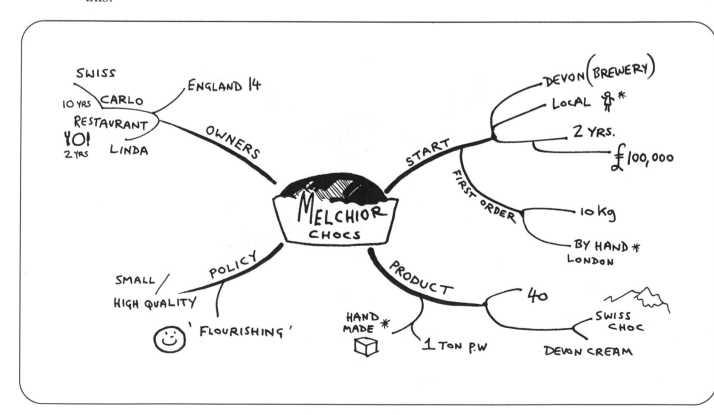

Challenge

Use Suggestion B the next time you teach any lesson involving information-gathering from reference sources (newspapers, text books, video programmes, lectures, internet).

Ponder Point...

In the early twelfth century, Hugh of St. Victor, instructing some young students on how to remember, explains clearly the mnemonic utility of manuscript page layout and decoration.

"It is a great value for fixing a memory-image that when we read books, we study to impress on our memory...the colour, shape, position, and placement of the letters...in what location (at the top, the middle or bottom) we saw [something] positioned....in what colour we observed the trace of the letter or the ornamented surface of the parchment. Indeed I consider nothing so useful for stimulating the memory as this."

Much later, a fifteenth-century French writer gives similar advice for fixing the text as a visual image in memory:

"Wherefore one best learns by studying from illuminated books, for the different colours bestow remembrance of the different lines and consequently of that thing which one wants to get by heart."

Challenge

Recall the 25 words from the "cat in a tree' story (Page 49). Try to decide how much you rely on pictures (in your head or on the page) to do this.

TEXT AS A PICTURE

Channel Tunnel visit - Polylogue

FF   This is what I like to see!
Ideas becoming reality - history in the making.

GG   You must be joking!
It's a terrible sight.
This was a beautiful valley a few years ago.
Now it's just railway lines, ugly bridges, and horrible buildings.

AA   I agree it's not beautiful to look at,
but you must admit it's a great engineering achievement.
They've levelled the site, dug the tunnels, laid the tracks,
and finished the terminal facilities.

GG   What a waste!
All this good farming land put under concrete,
Just think of the damage to the environment!

FF   You can't hold back progress.
The Tunnel is making a big difference to transport.
Distribution of goods will be much easier in future.
It's a great opportunity for business.
A lot of new companies will move into the area.

GG   I'm not sure that's entirely a good thing.
I'm afraid all the land to the side of the rail link to London
will become an industrial corridor.

AA   There are such a lot of new buildings around.
Passenger facilities, loading platforms, control towers.
I heard the whole thing cost £10.5 billion!
How did they get all that money?
From the French and English governments?

FF   No. It's privately funded, by banks and shareholders.

AA   There's still a lot of information I need to find out.

GG   What do you want to know?

AA   The answers to all the basic questions.
What are the dimensions of the Tunnel?
How long did it take to build? Construction techniques and so on.

EE   I've got most of the details in this leaflet.
The tunnel is 50km long - 40 km of that is below sea level.
Five thousand tunnel workers dug round the clock in shifts
They used eleven giant boring machines costing £7.5 m each!!
Work stated in 1987, and the Tunnel opened in April '95.

AA   Thanks. I'd also like to find out more about the types of trains - and I'm
interested in profitability, market share and so forth.

FF   I can help you with that.
But first. How about a cup of coffee in the café?

Three people are visiting the site of the Channel Tunnel. Join them on a windy hill top in South-East England. The sea is in the distance, but immediately below them is a large complex layout of tracks, platforms, passenger facilities, and all the paraphernalia of an enormous railway station.
FF- Fred Fastbuck is a property developer and wealthy businessman.
GG- Georgina Greenpeace is a Conservationist interested in the environment.
AA-Andrew Article is a Journalist writing a piece on European transport systems.
Choose to be one of these three characters; then read through the text.

This is an information text presented as a polylogue. There are a number of advantages. The most obvious is in **visual appeal**. Then there is the impact of direct speech. This gives an immediate opportunity to **dramatise** information. The role-play element links text to opinion, and provides scope for discussion. The memory map attached is an excellent way of reviewing the content of the polylogue and working through it 'gap-filling' mentally – cross-checking, linking the phrases and pictures.

Channel Tunnel visit – Memory Map

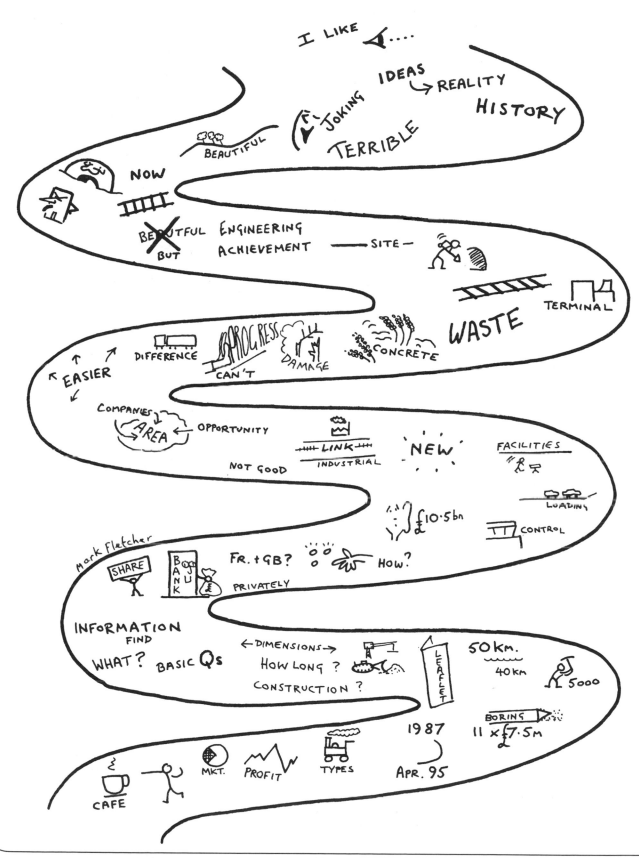

CHANGING PERSPECTIVES

A night at the opera

This is another way of changing perspectives.

As teachers, we get used to seeing things from familiar angles, to setting tasks in the expected manner.

However, tonight, at the Opera, we're seeing the great **Placido Donutto** from many different viewpoints.

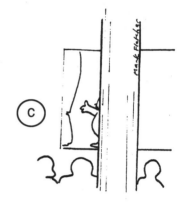

Which view do these people get?

1 Conductor	☐
2 Leading lady	☐
3 Lighting engineer	☐
4 Stage hand	☐
5 Placido himself	☐
6 Programme seller	☐
7 Occupant of cheapest seat	☐
8 Lady in 3rd row of stalls	☐

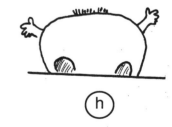

Challenge

Is there a task activity you use which could be taken from a different perspective which would then fire more student imagination and creativity?

In the world of Sport, top players have their own ways of 'psyching up' for the game. "I always visualise success on the pitch", says one England rugby international. "I see the actions on the pitch with my own eyes and feel myself being there, then I visualise the perfect piece of play taking place in front of me. I go into the mind-set". Another key forward says, "Before a big game I do my stretching, visualise a move and what my role is and visualise it going well, then relax."

"Nerves and butterflies in your stomach are fine - they're a physical sign that you're mentally ready and eager. You have to get the butterflies to fly in formation, that's the trick! You have to train your nerves to get into the ideal mental state by focusing on goals."

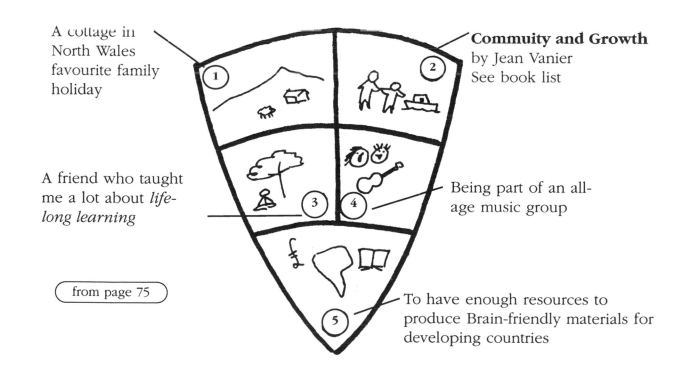

A cottage in North Wales favourite family holiday

Commuity and Growth
by Jean Vanier
See book list

A friend who taught me a lot about *life-long learning*

Being part of an all-age music group

from page 75

To have enough resources to produce Brain-friendly materials for developing countries

MORE VISUALISATION
Lesson Planning

This time - let's visualise the lesson as a meal.

Think about levels of formality.

A **banquet** is formal - a teacher-centred set piece. A high degree of organisation is required. Guests are invited and the stages of the meal are carefully structured and initiated. There are certain key moments, often prepared speeches in formal register. Diners see the menu, know the purpose of the meal and its stages, and what is expected of them. The meal is served to the guests. The seating plan controls the range of interaction and communication.

A **buffet** party is different. There is plenty of variety on offer. People help themselves, loading their plates with certain things, avoiding other things, perhaps being disappointed if they're at the back of the queue. In the class situation, learner independence perhaps works very well for the organised student who knows what she wants. Everything is less formal than at the banquet, people chat in groups or circulate, drink in hand. Sometimes at a meal like this the host provides a certain amount of food but each guest contributes a tasty, speciality dish.

SELF SERVICE

BUFFET

How about a **child's birthday party**? There is certainly a lot of noisy, excited interaction - games coordinated to a greater or lesser extent and the highlight of blowing out candles on the cake. There's usually a lot of emotional ups and downs. The tablecloth will need a good wash afterwards. Effort goes into providing a limited range of always popular things to eat and almost certainly guests will go home with a goody bag of sticky edibles. Some participants will feel exhausted afterwards even if they've had a good time.

A children's birthday party

Lesson Planning (continued)

Some meals are very much quicker and require very little preparation. Nevertheless, they may be exactly right for the moment. The hastily grabbed coffee and piece of bread for **breakfast**, gulped down as the mind races ahead on affairs of the day (or struggles to shake off torpor). Is the hasty dash to the photocopier an example of up-to-the-moment inspiration, or sheer lack of planning and commitment?

Then there's the **dinner party** for friends, **tea** with the in-laws, a **picnic** . . . and so on.

Just as we enjoy many different types of meal, we need a variety of types of lesson - formal input, improvisation, learner choice.....

Recall in detail a lesson you taught recently.
Visualise the situation - room/students/yourself/materials/staging/activities/response.

Think of that lesson as a meal. Which type is it most like? Did everyone enjoy it? Did anyone get indigestion (or food poisoning)? How was it prepared and served? Who served it? How did guests show their appreciation? Was there something for auditory and visual and kinaesthetic eaters (as well as the olfactory and gustatory ones, of course). Think of a week of lessons. Are they similar types of meal - or quite different 'eating experiences'?

WHAT'S ON THE MENU?

Ponder Point...

Choose a lesson you are going to teach in the next few days. What is your chosen lesson most like? – tea with the in-laws? a picnic? a formal banquet?

What's on the menu for the   V (Visual)
                                         A (Auditory)
                                         K (Kinaesthetic) learner?

DO-IT-YOURSELF CLASSROOM PICASSO

Developing Skills

There are lots of teaching skills I need to work on,
and many situations where I have little or no
experience and would struggle to survive.
That's probably true for all of us.
One thing I can do reasonably well is drawing
little pictures.
The next few pages are simple tips to encourage
anyone who thinks *"I can't draw"*. (Usually because at
age four some absolute clot made a disparaging remark about
your play-school picture of an orange and has left a scar for
life!)

I have two left feet, and think of myself
as totally unpractical for the same reason.

Scarred for life!

The trick with classroom drawing is to do a few
things VERY FAST. That means minimum detail;
and lines which make a difference! We're not in
the Sistine Chapel ceiling business here.
Cartoonists know that **we see what we expect
to see** (most of the time) so a lot of classroom
drawing comes down to control of a few
stereotypes (and lots of practice!)

Challenge

When you have worked through the next few pages, decide what
special gift you have - and how your colleagues can benefit from it.

D.I.Y. PICASSO
Facial expressions

What makes the difference?

Do It Yourself

Here are five other key expressions to practise.

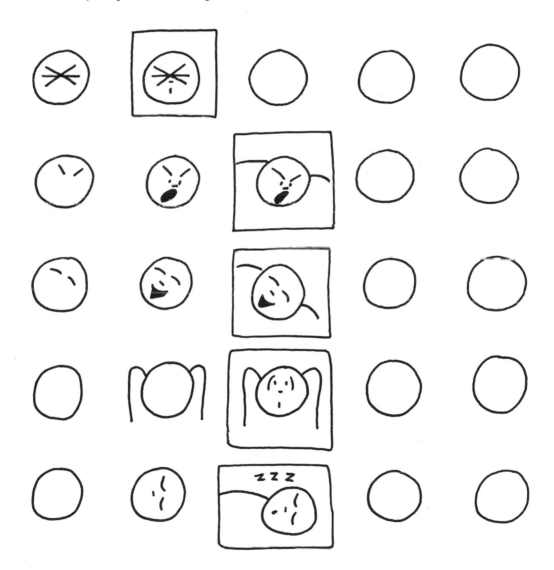

Mark Fletcher   Teaching for Success   English Experience

D.I.Y PICASSO
Figures
What makes the difference?

We have 3 people.

A child,

a teenager,

and an adult.

What makes the difference?

now we have a relationship

and a setting

... and a time, and some weather and the possibility

of a huge variety of stories !

What's just happened? What's going to happen?

D.I.Y. PICASSO
Men and Women

What makes the difference?
(in classroom drawing)

 same

   same

  same

  *different*

The rest is decoration!

and very useful . . .

Here is **Miss Scribble** going shopping

. . . and at a dinner party.

Challenge ────────────────────────────

Bring her to life at the party
– without taking your pen from the paper!

D.I.Y PICASSO

What makes the difference?

Challenge

In the space below have a go at drawing . . .
– a family having a picnic - when *something happens!*

Challenge

Choose a simple cartoon character and use it as your signature?

Mind Map

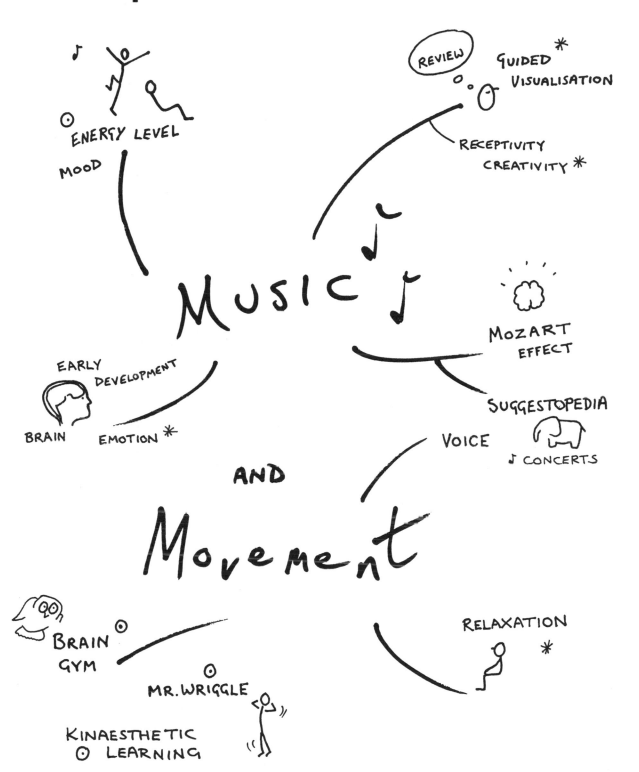

ENERGY LEVEL

MOOD

REVIEW

GUIDED *
VISUALISATION

RECEPTIVITY
CREATIVITY *

MUSIC

MOZART
EFFECT

EARLY
DEVELOPMENT

BRAIN   EMOTION *

SUGGESTOPEDIA

VOICE

♪ CONCERTS

AND

Movement

BRAIN
GYM

RELAXATION
*

MR. WRIGGLE

KINAESTHETIC
⊙ LEARNING

Ponder Point...

Movement is a child's first language.
(Sally Goddard Blythe- Co-Director,
Inst. for Neuro-Physiological Psychology, Chester)

Ponder Point...

Music is a language without words. In common with
other languages it imposes order, structure, rhythm,
timing and sound frequency discrimination. It gives
meaning to sound. It is one of life's earliest natural teachers.
(Sally Goddard Blythe)

Ponder Point...

So, when we plan our education we must consider
what effect we wish to produce in our learners,
and choose our music, our literature, our poetry,
our dance, our harmonies so that they will
produce that effect. *(Plato and Socrates)*

MUSIC & MOVEMENT

Even before birth, we respond to music. A foetus's hearing develops in the womb and is the means by which it begins to sense the outside world. The brain evolves using the principles of melody, rhythm and dynamics in order to develop thought, consciousness and emotion.

Music has been shown to reach people who are severely distressed or disabled physically, mentally or emotionally. It seems that the part of the brain that responds to music remains intact even after a trauma to other areas of the body – giving music the potential to heal. We are very familiar with the uses of music to create a mood in films, and to excite at sports events or calm in dentists' waiting rooms.

Sound is the main sensory stimulus for the foetus in the womb. Our neurology develops in constant interaction with sound. Our culture is dominated by visual images - but we also recognise the vital role of sound, and of the auditory system which gives us our sense of balance. Understanding more about how our brain responds to sound, and the resulting emotional effect of sound on us, will make a crucial contribution to discussions of learning and teaching. Earlier (page 13) we identified 'auditory' as one of the main learning styles. Let's look a little more closely at the brain and music.

'Hearing' is our auditory system sensing a wide range of molecular vibration. The speed of the vibrations determines how high or low they sound - their 'pitch'. Music is the ordering of pitched sounds. In brain terms, certain relationships of sounds produce symmetrical patterns as they activate neurons. We respond to these as 'harmonious'. Other relationships create asymmetric firing patterns and we respond to these as 'discordant'. Our auditory system is superbly created to monitor continually and subconsciously the complex multi-dimensional sound world that surrounds us. It enables us to infer the source, speed, location of all these auditory stimuli. Our left and right ears are linked to the opposite hemisphere of the brain (page 10) but it seems that the left ear 'prefers' lower notes, and the right 'prefers' higher notes. Location of a sound and perception of pitch are functions of different brain areas, and we realise once again the diversity and complexity of the neurological systems contributing to our coherent sound-picture of the world.

PET scans (page 15) show that listening to, interpreting, responding to music activates areas of the right hemisphere, which is associated with emotion and meaning. This is an inherent neurological response which we all have. Another interesting observation is that music stimulates activity in the occipital lobes - an area particularly associated with visualisation (page 12). Music stimulates this area even when our eyes are closed. So, as teachers, we can begin to develop a rationale for using music and relaxation in the context of, for example, guided visualisation. By engaging the emotions at a deep level, and enhancing the student's own ability to create pictures in the mind's eye, music provides access to rich sources of imagination.

Music carries meaning and the brain's response to that meaning shows in right hemisphere activity. Language is primarily a left hemisphere function (page 10) but the right hemisphere also becomes involved when words carry emotional meaning. Music has a role in synthesing brain activity because it acts on so many different areas simultaneously. Repetitive rhythms are probably connected to the ancient 'Reptilian' brain. In the limbic system, auditory input is directly associated with memory, feelings, mood. The highly developed frontal lobes process intellectual pleasure in musical form. Their sophisticated responses to music include imagination, creativity and personality development.

What is the 'Mozart effect'? American researchers investigating how neurons trigger connections in the brain, converted print-outs of neurons firing into sounds. The sound sequences formed seemed similar to tonal classical music. Subsequent pilot studies showed students performed better in abstract reasoning tests after listening to Mozart for ten minutes. Can this be true? If so, the implications for teachers and parents are enormous. It's early days to make sweeping generalisations, but at least it's possible to see why, in brain terms, there might be a learning benefit from working with music. Our auditory system is constantly involved in anticipating and finding patterns in order to make sense of the world around. Supremely, but in common with similar composers, the music of Mozart weaves wonderful patterns into satisfying and delightful emotional experiences. When it comes to starting other learning tasks, the brain which has been engaged in listening to these musical patterns could well be 'up-and-running', with many brain regions already linking efficiently, and so could be in excellent condition to tackle new challenges!

Ponder Point...

It was Pythagoras who first discerned the link between mathematics and music and showed how those notes which the ear perceives as being harmonious are divisible by whole numbers. Those mathematical rules of harmony are the basis of so much great painting, music and architecture. This is the methodology of art and it is a methodology which is especially effective and affective in teaching.
(*Robert Gillan- former Director of SEAL*)

I always have at least two cassettes on hand when I am teaching. One is very bright jazz to give people a lift as they come into class tired or distracted, and the other is some Baroque largos to establish a calm, unifying atmosphere. My experience also suggests that Peruvian flute music is universally acceptable as a musical way of doing this, but you will have your own ideas as to what is appropiate for your classes.

I use background music during pair work activities. It signals a harmonious, non-threatening atmosphere. I also use it as a pedagogic tool for suggestopedic concert readings of text (see The Suggestopedic Elephant on page 84). Any text read while following lively classical music will alert the brain to expectations of something special. The teacher's voice can emphasise key target information by pauses or changes in volume.

Time spent on facilitating a relaxed state before a Guided Visualisation or concert reading is well spent in terms of outcome - and often, in our rushed lives, welcome and therapeutic. People are most receptive to intuitive insights when the body is relaxed and the mind is free from internal chatter. Students do need to know what's going on, however, and why. There is lots of scope for 'seeing what works'. Some people in a group may have genuine objections that a piece of music is intrusive, or has particular unwelcome associations for them. These objections have to be respected.

When working with adult learners, it is more than likely some will have relaxation techniques of their own. If this is the case, they can lead the class through the exercises (instead of the teacher being centre stage). Using such opportunities is a great boost to student confidence, and we should create them whenever we can.

Below is a short list of some pieces of music which have been specifically recommended by Dr Lozanov for suggestopedic concert readings.

Active Concert

Mozart
Concerto for Violin and Orchestra
Symphony No. 40 in G minor KV550
Haydn
Symphony 101 in C Major
Symphony 94 in G Major
Brahms
Concerto for Violin and
Orchestra in D Major, op.77

Passive Concert

Corelli	*Concerti grossi, op.6, No. 4, 10, 11, 12*
Vivaldi	*Five Concerti for Flute and Chamber*
	Orchestra (G Major, F Major, G Minor, C Major)
Albinoni	*Sinfonia in G*
Pachebel	*Canon in D*

The Society for Affective Effective Learning (SEAL) publishes a Bibliography which gives details of research; see page 144.

Ponder Point...

"Singing and dancing should be integrated into the daily routine in every school every day. It creates the basis for intellectual development. Music draws upon feeling and thinking, joining the emotional with the rational. It brings out the best in a child or young adult."
Yehudi Menuhin

RELAXATION EXERCISE

Relax . . .

..find a good sitting position. Sit comfortably with your back well supported, and your head well balanced.

Close your eyes and listen to the music.

Tighten your muscles. Then relax them.

Breathe deeply and steadily.

Wrinkle, then relax your forehead.

Your body rhythm has slowed. Your mind is calm and receptive.

· ·

To 'come back' . . .

Wriggle your fingers,

Roll your shoulders.

and your toes.

Slowly turn your head to look around. Smile! Then have a big S-T-R-E-T-C-H.

LESSON REVIEW
relaxation and visualisation

Reading through the main points to very gentle music, is a marvellously refreshing end to a lesson, or day, and is really appreciated by students. The body is 'passive' but the mind is taking in information peripherally. Do try this as a way of recycling/consolidating teaching input. Students need to know that they can relax (see previous page) and that there will be no comprehension question follow-up. All they need to do is to listen to the music, and allow the information to gently echo in the mind with no conscious effort.

I've demonstrated and discussed this technique with many teachers in three different continents who have all found it valuable. One illuminating comment which struck me was that "students find it quite therapeutic to take time in the rush of school life to just sit and be 'centred' - and so do I!"

When the participants are relaxed, talk through the target information points of the lesson as the music plays.

A refinement is to transport participants to a pleasant scene – a beach, sunny woodland, spring garden – and attach positive sensory experiences to the visualised scene. For example,

"You are walking along a beautiful sandy beach. See the colours in your Mind's Eye. Feel the warm sunshine, and listen to the gentle sounds of the waves. Feel the sand between your toes and the salt on your lips.
Stop for a moment. Breathe in,- and enjoy the experience of this place.
There are some attractive shells on the beach. Choose one and pick it up.
Notice the colours and how good it feels in your hand. Hold the shell to your ear. You will hear the sea,- and also the main points of our lesson again....

Add the review of the lesson here.

Enjoy the moment, the colours, the warmth. The lesson content will always be available to you when you return to this place in your imagination, and pick up your special shell, and listen again.
It's almost time to return. As you walk back along the beach, continue to enjoy the experience - you can bring it back with you!

And now, wriggle your fingers and your toes, your hands and feet.
Roll your shoulders.Take a deep breath, open your eyes, and have a big S-T-R-E-T-C-H.
Look around and smile at the people near you. Stamp your feet on the floor.
Welcome back!"

(The Power of Metaphor (Michael Berman – Crown House) has further examples of this technique)

TAKING CARE OF YOUR VOICE

How we feel affects our voice, and this has a big impact on the reactions, in particular the expectations, of our listeners. Low self-esteem caused by feeling 'disconnected' can affect voice quality. Energy drains from the speaker, and from the listener. A harsh voice can create negative reactions.

Here are a few tips on servicing one of the teacher's vital assets!

- Develop some voice 'warm-up' routines. Start with some 'yawns' to stretch the back of your throat. Hum, then sing, up and down a scale. 'Loosen up' by gently massaging cheeks and neck while you do this. 'Chant' the vowels...do that again making high resonating 'head' notes, 'nasal' notes. Run through the vowel sounds again changing volume.

- Practise relaxing - generally, and especially the muscles of face, shoulders, neck (tension prevents free breathing).

DOH
RAY
ME
FAH

- Get into the habit of monitoring how your voice 'is'. Does it have lots of energy and a variety of volume, colour, tone, pitch. Make a conscious effort to vary your delivery.

- Try not to over-use your voice. Look for voice 'rest breaks' in the lesson and have liquids available.

- Avoid straining to shout over the top of classroom noise. Do this by having a signal (little bell or similar) for when you want students to be quieten down. Have a follow-up signal for complete quiet.

- Work on techniques for giving instructions clearly and just once, not repeating them six times! (Remember the Visual and Kinaesthetic learners).

- Start as you mean to go on by arriving in class with positive energy - not necessarily bouncing around, but conveying the message that the lesson is going to be valuable, and, if you really are feeling low.....fake it till you make it !

Ponder Point...

Dr. Alfred Tomatis has shown that chanting, such as that done regularly by monks, whilst it sounds very low to our ears, generates high frequency sound. This energises the brain and contributes to stamina.

BRAIN GYM

Linking left and right hemispheres ...

These Brain gym exercises, also known as Educational Kinaesthetics, were developed by Paul and Gail Dennison. They are simple and popular for raising energy, dealing with stress and getting ready for focused working. The Dennisons claim that the exercises integrate the left and right hemispheres of the brain by physical movements. Here are some...

★ **Brain buttons** Stand up. Put one hand on your navel. With the thumb and one finger of the other hand find and rub the small hollows just below the collar bone (increases clarity for visual activity, such as reading).

★ **Cross crawl** Stand up. Rhythmically touch the left knee with your right hand and then the right knee with your left. When that rhythm is going nicely, put a little more effort into the exercise by using your elbows instead of your hands. (Right hemisphere controls left side movement and vice-versa. This activity coordinates the two and gets them working together.)

★ **The Owl** Squeeze the muscles of the left shoulder with your right hand while looking over the left shoulder, pulling your shoulders back and breathing deeply. Drop your chin to your chest, breathe deeply again. Reverse the movement. (Releases tension from sitting and improves concentration.)

★ **Cook's hook ups** (first stage) Put left ankle over right knee. Grasp ball of left foot with left hand and hold left ankle with right hand. Sit for a minute, eyes closed, breathing deeply, tongue on roof of mouth.

(second stage) Uncross legs. Put finger tips together. Continue to breathe deeply for another minute. (Diffuses stress and establishes a state of readiness for learning)

You will find the Brain Gym reference in the book list on page 144.

Quite separate from that, but making an appearance here anyway is...

'Mr. Wriggle'. Every twenty minutes or so Mr. Wriggle comes in to the classroom and gives permission for everyone to stand up, move, stretch, scratch, have a quick shoulder massage for twenty seconds, - and then get back to work feeling re-energised.

Drinking plenty of **water** is recommended - headaches can be caused by dehydration. Water conducts electricity and, of course, our brains function with electrical impulses.

Ponder Point... A colleague who uses Brain gym a lot with her primary classes said that she had recently seen three children who were unable to do very simple 'cross crawl' exercises. She was worried that this lack of coordination might have resulted from prolonged and sedentary entertainment via the TV and computer screens from an early age. If this were to be the case, then Brain gym or its equivalent becomes even more of an imperative.

The Way Forward

CHANGING OBSTACLES INTO OPPORTUNITIES

We have discussed key information on brain functions, memory and learning styles, surveyed affective approaches, and thought about ways of enriching learning possibilities with music, movement and visuals. It would be surprising if, in the course of reading this book, you hadn't come across an appealing idea but felt it would be difficult to introduce it in your teaching situation. A 'Yes, but ....' These 'obstacles' are natural self-defence mechanisms. They cannot be 'battered down' by a zealous teacher. They can only be dismantled, healthily and safely, by you, the individual, when you find they are no longer needed.

The classroom as a whole needs...

- A very supportive atmosphere with pair and group work, encouragement, positive expectations, and 'mistakes' seen as steps on the ladder to success.
- Clear indications that the students are aware (at an appropriate level) of a 'BRAIN-*friendly*' rationale for the way they are working, and are participating willingly.
- The teacher's obvious sensitivity to learning styles and the provision for different types of learner, with plenty of opportunities for 'recycling' language.
- Opportunities for students to see how each lesson fits into the big picture.
- Opportunities for students to contribute by sharing their knowledge (and uncertainties).
- Creativity which can be through movement, use of colour, drama, role-play, songs, games, or visuals.
- Different brainwave patterns, possibly established through music, or working on information at different levels. Some lively and interactive phases and others of calm, 'passive' review.
- A buzz of enthusiasm because learners realise they are experiencing real progress, and know they have the strategies for remembering the new material, and move on further.

YESBUT *Hold on a moment! That sounds great, but I have to go into a cramped and ugly room where I can't move furniture or put anything on the walls. I have forty-five minutes twice a week with a large group of teenagers who have to take my compulsory subject (Physics / French / Maths). It's a bit different from the ideal world you are describing!*

You are right, of course. You clearly feel you can't make much of an impact on the external learning environment – but certainly you can go a considerable way towards optimising the students' *internal* learning environment.
Be the teacher who always brings into the classroom something different and interesting. Don't labour the point, but have a 'surprise object' for display, have pictures, diagrams or quotations, which are colourful and can quickly be fixed to the wall and easily removed. Pause outside the door, gather yourself, and bring an instant 'high interest' charge into the room with you.

You probably can't improve the timetable in the short term. It might be possible, however, to find like-minded colleagues and work towards double periods, or hour-long sessions where the benefits of different levels of brainwave activity can really be explored and enjoyed. Use music as a background to establish a calming, or an energetic, atmosphere. Once this is accepted, introduce 'quiet music' times near the end of a lesson when students listen as you recap the main points. When *that* is accepted, move on to left-right hemisphere linking activities such as reading texts suggestopedically with music.

YESBUT *I'd need a lot of confidence before trying something like that with my classes. They're used to very traditional methods. I really don't know where to start.*

It's a matter of establishing a point of contact, of trust. With my disaffected apprentice motor mechanics, pressured back into school for remedial English, we started with an argument about the most popular cars, then moved to a video of the 'high-tech' Toyota assembly line and a shot of employees taking an energetic stretch break in the middle of their shift. This raised questions about efficiency, and led for the first time to the voluntary opening of a window!

A discussion with remand prisoners on 'dropping out of school' led to a comparison of teachers' methods, and personal learning styles. For some, this brought a realisation that they had not 'failed' because of intrinsic stupidity, but perhaps because teachers had never presented the subject in a way they could relate to. See AVK awareness on page 38.

This insight brought the beginnings of renewed self-esteem and a real chance to 'break the mould'.

Whatever the class situation, there is always a connecting point with the 'BRAIN-*friendly*' ideas which allows the first step to be taken. Why does an airline play soft music on take-off? Why do you remember one advert more than another? Why is it so difficult to pass a jigsaw puzzle without pausing to fit in one more piece?

Your learners will soon recognise that we constantly apply the same understandings in every successful sphere of life. Take your learners into your confidence and they will rapidly produce similar fascinating observations of their own.

YESBUT *I teach adult business people who have the attitude that they are there to learn – which will be hard, serious work – and I am there to teach – which certainly doesn't mean 'playing games' or 'fooling around'.*

Business people will recognise that the 'BRAIN-*friendly*' revolution is actually 'industry-driven'. Human Resource managers in top companies are amongst those most keenly interested and active in this field because they need to retrain staff rapidly as job demands change.

Build your own confidence by examining how the activities you already use have their rationale in the context of the 6-point 'BRAIN-*friendly*' checklist. See page 16. Work on your own strategies for being relaxed, organised, and unflustered.

Be clear about your aims, and share with the group how each lesson fits into the big picture of their progress. Be prepared to offer a 'left brain' logical explanation if you are challenged on the validity of a 'right brain' activity. Use pair work, non-threatening tasks which appeal to the limbic system and appropriate humour as you build a supportive team atmosphere in the group. Collect a data base of authoritative books, articles and references which will demonstrate the good sense behind what you are doing.

YESBUT *My groups are younger, and working for an exam. They and their parents demand good grades. There just isn't time, in the few lessons we have, to do anything but try to get through the coursebook and complete the syllabus.*

I sympathise, and it's counter-productive to attempt to turn all expectations upside down overnight by imposing a totally new approach. If you are extremely time-pressured and exam- coursebook- constrained (and many teachers are) remember that your students, like you, have at least a hundred billion (10 to the power 11) brain cells each, and that each one of these cells can connect with up to ten thousand others.

Look at the possibility of using mind maps for notetaking with listening tasks, a card system for systematic revision, a coloured 'highlighter' culture for emphasising key information, music to help establish an optimum energy level, multi-sensory imaging to engage the right hemisphere and bring texts to life.

Parents and students alike will be won over to 'BRAIN-*friendly*' methods because they produce happier, involved participants with improved results!

YESBUT *I know students who are really afraid to 'let go' and risk becoming committed to a more creative style of learning.*

Keep on presenting opportunities, but don't try to force people. Be especially considerate where cultural factors may be an issue.

My own confidence in the 'BRAIN-*friendly*' revolution was given a tremendous boost by a right-handed lady who constantly reiterated that she couldn't draw (during a 'Visuals Linked to Language' session). Eight days later her confidence in herself and what the group was doing had so improved that she began to draw beautifully – with the left hand she had been shamed into not using some fifty years earlier. Her brain had in some wonderful way reasserted her right to a skill which had been denied her by years of negative comment.

Quite shy students will often change their self-image and become willing to 'have a go' if there are props or masks available for role play. As teachers, we need skills to encourage self-development – and a plentiful supply of patience!

YESBUT *My teaching colleagues are very suspicious of attempts to introduce new ideas. They think it undermines the good work they're already doing.*

This can be a real problem. However, 'the proof of the pudding is in the eating', and be assured that all over the world teachers are becoming involved in the 'BRAIN-*friendly* revolution'.

If you have a local teachers' organisation, you will certainly be able to find some kindred spirits who want to relate such possibilities to specific situations. How about joining an organisation such as SEAL (see page 145 for details) – an educational charity with a wealth of networking experience?

Meanwhile, begin collecting your data base of supportive authority. Take the steps (perhaps as simple as my trainee mechanics opening a window!) which do not threaten colleagues.

Give value to the things which others do which are successful before going public with your own more radical developments. Keep healthy, keep enquiring, keep a sense of humour – and keep persevering.

Barriers **do** get removed and doors **do** open!

'The proof of the pudding ....'

Ponder Point...

The future is not inevitable. We can influence it if we know what we want it to be.   *Charles Handy*

CHOOSING AND MANAGING YOUR TOP TEAM

Sports fans in the UK (and I'm sure those elsewhere) will be familiar with the 'fantasy team' competitions in which thousands of participants pick players for their ideal team and are credited with points depending on how those players perform week by week in their leagues. I'm going to introduce a combination of stars for my **Teaching-for-Success** squad and invite you to consider your own selection.

Each of us brings to our teaching a wonderful range of received wisdom, hard-won experience and cherished intuitions. These insights complement and play off each other at a subconscious level every time we go into a classroom or even think about the job we do. Here are some key members of my Brain-friendly 'teaching team' but I would emphasise that they are parts of a 'whole' and have most value when they 'play' together.

As the teacher, I'm responsible for 'managing' this team, monitoring performance and making sure that there is a place for the rising new 'stars' being signed up in the course of my own development. (The team has 11 players but, happily, any number of immensely valuable reserves can be brought on to add specialist skills!)

Here's one of our key players, **Rita Rationale.**

She always plays on the left side of the field. Her first job is to make it clear that there is an excellent, justifiable reason for each of our players to hold their place in the team. She has developed a playing style which is strong on clear aims and carefully thought-out procedures. She underpins the vital areas of syllabus design, lesson planning, classroom methodology, feedback, with an approach which meets all professional standards. The part played by every other member of the side can also be explained pedagogically, although several of her team-mates really have to be seen (or better still experienced) to be believed! Personally, she's best at logical, analytical skills. For every lesson she wants to know, *'What can the students do when they leave the room that they couldn't do when they arrived?'* She needs to be clear about the aim of each lesson – and she needs to know how far that aim has been achieved.

Our key mid-field player is **Chris (Corpus) Colossum.** He keeps the balance in the team by ensuring that while left hemisphere players organise structured programmes and systematically check on training and progress, right field team-mates have the freedom to develop more intuitive, inspirational moves.

This way he gives **Mike Memory** match-winning opportunities to turn short-term gains into long-term benefits. Mike is an expert on study skills tactics. Some of these ploys are very left brain (for example, lesson planning which considers 'attention spans' and 'regular revisions') whilst others, such as mind-mapping, colour-coding, contextualising, involve more right brain moves.

In goal we have **Sam Security**. Sam has come to prominence through the limbic system. She inspires the sort of confidence which allows learners to experiment and take risks without the fear of looking foolish. With Sam in goal, learners know that if they miss things or make mistakes it is not a disaster. This need of Security, of course, runs through every learning situation – primary pupils, exam-facing teenagers, recently-arrived refugees, job-pressurised business people. Sam represents the teacher's professional competence but also has the caring attitude, and the skills, to encourage mutual support amongst the class.

Linking closely with Sam it's good to have **Leonora Learning-Environment** in the team. Leonora excels in optimising physical conditions in the classroom. Can everyone see and hear comfortably? How easy is it for teacher and students to move around? Is the temperature/fresh air supply good for working? Is the room as interesting and attractive as it can be? Are interruptions and frustrations reduced to the minimum, and can students contribute something to make this 'their' learning

space? Since she is also a product of the limbic system she works in the area of maintaining successful internal learning states. Anything that might disturb learners emotionally, ethically (*'That offends me!'*), or logically (*'That doesn't make sense!'*) needs to be tackled before barriers go up and a 'fight or flight' reaction blocks learning. Leonora not only monitors lessons closely but thinks carefully about the composition of working groups, how to correct most effectively, developing strategies to integrate 'difficult' students, and other sensitive, affective, issues.

Since this is a team effort, part of Leonora's success comes from the close understanding developed with **Adrian Van Kneebone**, who delivers information in ways which appeal to the different learning strengths of other players. Adrian's pre-match instructions to you regarding this section of **Teaching for Success** would be to:

a. make your own mind map of it (illustrated of course);

b. record a version of it as a conversation between players, then listen as you i) cycle to work ii) lie in the bath;

c. play the little matching game which appears in the half-time slot;

d. dip the page in warm chocolate and chew it reflectively (not sure about that one!).

Seriously though, do think through one of your recent lessons and consider carefully what it contained for the Visual, the Auditory and the Kinaesthetic learner. If you were teaching that lesson again tomorrow, would you alter the balance at all?

As you might guess, **Vera Visualise** is a tower of strength in this type of review/planning activity. She enables the teacher to run through an 'internal movie' of a lesson and observe what happened / might happen.

In this way strategies can be introduced to intercept potential problems and maximise benefit. A simple example is to visualise students taking part in a future communicative exercise in order to anticipate what props/room organisation would make it more engaging, and what 'input' would increase the 'pay off'. Another of Vera's tactics is to teach students to create their own image of people and places mentioned in a text. (This is easily done with a set of open questions – a visualisation ladder.) By investing their own imagination in the situation a new relationship is established with the text. Motivation increases, and the associated information becomes more meaningful and more memorable!

It's time for a half-time break so get up, stretch, and have half an orange! You have met seven of my team. When you are ready, meet the other four players and the coach and add them to the team profile too.

Challenge

Look back at the profiles and match the names to the descriptions in the Team Profile below (and draw them!). One box is completed as an example.

TEAM PROFILE

Name	Name	Name	Name
	Leonora Learning Environment		
○ Midfield player, linking R & L	○ Midfield player, Always in peak condition	○ Very adaptable, plays in a number of styles	○ Totally reliable in defence

Name	Name	Name	Name
○ Dreams up great new moves	○ Natural planner and strategist	○ Never forgets a useful tactic	○ A real dynamo

Name	Name	Name	Name
○ A brilliant motivator	○ Always relaxed never stressed	○ The joker of the team	○ Modest – but great at beating defences

Alongside Vera, on the right hand side of the field is **Percival Peripheral**. Percy never attracts the headlines. His secret skill is being so unobtrusive that he can ease through defensive learning blocks. Quite small cues displayed in the room (wall charts/pictures/student work/key words/ phrases/objects) will trigger associations with work already done and serve to reactivate memory traces. It is not necessary to draw attention to these cues. They will be noticed at a subconscious level and can serve also to plant seeds of interest for a lesson which is to come.

Operating with similar aims but playing with a very different style is **Freda Fun 'n' Games**. A lot of learning takes place while attention is focused on the outcome of a game, or on friendly competition to solve a puzzle. Freda might give the impression of being very 'laid back' in her approach but don't be misled. She's actually very focused and highly organised. Even the 'stretch breaks' which she disguises as changes of grouping, students coming to the board to write, jazz chants, etc., are there not just for subject practice or class management interest, but to activate the reflex brain through movement, and to raise energy levels through laughter.

The twins, **Alison Active** and **Penny Passive** are trained in Suggestopedia. Fascinating research is leading to the conclusion that humans are intrinsically musical. The metaphor of Western medical science which has the body as a mechanism to be taken apart, repaired and reassembled may be less helpful than an emerging understanding of body, mind and emotion as a kind of symphonic composition. Music calls on widely dispersed areas of the brain, many of which lie beyond our usual consciousness.

Rhythmic components of music create specific physiological changes. These beneficial changes are becoming established in healing. An exciting area for us will be to see them become established in teaching. In our team, Alison Active is always very alert, following the interplay of words and music in language texts. Penny Passive on the other hand is much more relaxed and slows down the play to an Alpha brainwave state. She processes language without an intellectual filter so that it becomes directly part of the learner's experience.

Whereas Rita Rationale checks what has been learned by asking concept questions and setting tests, Penny prefers to provide very calming, reflective musical interludes which review the lesson and give value to deeper processes of the brain without any expectation of instant response.

Every successful team has a good trainer. Ours is **Paul Positive**. Paul is very open-minded. He is always looking for ways to improve performance and raise the level of expectation of every player in the team. He finds strengths in every learner and builds on them so that each person knows they have a contribution of value to make. He provides study skills to encourage autonomous learning, but also works on a healthy dynamic within the class. He doesn't ignore mistakes but creates an atmosphere in which they are viewed not as failures but as steps on the way to success.

Well, that is my personal team selection. Twelve key concepts which derive from the 'BRAIN-*friendly*' package.

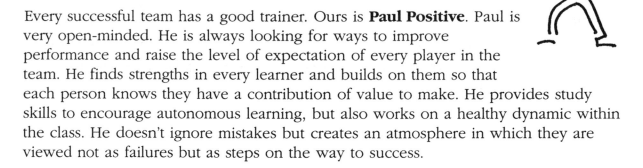

Challenge

There are lots of other excellent candidates for a place in the team. From your own teaching experience, what other 'stars' would you add to your own squad?

"TOP TIPS" GAME . . .

On the next pages is a list of teaching tips mainly gleaned from my conversations with numerous teachers. Some of the tips raise issues, some are very pragmatic, some might seem obvious and others won't make sense unless you've read the relevant bit in this book.

● **Step 1** Skim read the list (they are in no special order). Choose four different coloured felt tips and put either **CM** (classroom management), **BF** (BRAIN-friendly), **PP** (Personal protection) or **TD** (Teacher Development) against each. Of course they're bound to overlap - but which category seems closest?

● **Step 2** Pick out 4 tips for each category. Choose four that seem really important. Jot down the reference numbers.

● **Step 3** Add 4 more tips - either from this list or from your own practical experience. You now have twenty very valuable thoughts about **Teaching for Success.** How about:

– Making a colourful poster?

– Photocopying your list and inviting colleagues to comment or make their own?

– Putting the list where you will see it every day!

– Putting it on your/the school's website?

– Including it in a networking newsletter?

– Or indeed any variation of the activity which encourages fellow teachers and supports good practice.

Brain Joke answer:
"It's because the male brains *have hardly been used!*"   **(Sorry about that!)**

1   Check there is enough oxygen in the classroom.

2   Have water available.

3   Bring something 'different' into the lesson.

4   Have a tin of colours available.

5   Use colours on board/flip chart.

6   Have a 'props' bag.

7   Have a lively cassette available.

8   Have a slow, relaxing cassette available.

9   Read through the main points of the lesson to music.

10   Use visualisation to provide context.

11   Use visualisation ladders to enrich...

12   Use mind maps for comprehension texts.

13   Use mind maps for information exchange.

14   Check everyone in the class can see and hear.

15   Establish your 'position in room' for instructions.

16   Have a way of attracting attention which doesn't involve using your voice.

17   Check that students move quite frequently.

18   Introduce a 'Mr Wriggle' equivalent for stretch breaks. See page 122.

19   Learn/teach some Brain Gym.

20   Collect articles on the brain as 'Authority' for your methods.

21   Check your own learning preferences.

22   Make learning cards for subject areas.

23   Look for cartoons connected to your subject.

24   Investigate opportunities for systematic colour coding.

25   Have your lesson plan in mind map form.

26 Use colour on your lesson plan.

27 Choose and practise drawing a permanent cartoon figure.

28 Get quicker at drawing basic figures.

29 Have lozenges for your voice.

30 Use a variety of coloured paper for handouts.

31 Acquire a set of foolproof, positive, starter activities.

32 Make sure you give yourself time to close a lesson without rush.

33 Have ways to signal corrections without using your voice.

34 Be as organised as you can.

35 Relate every lesson to a context of the 'bigger picture'.

36 Think about pairings/composition of groups.

37 Consider putting information into story form or dramatised form.

38 Do the things that you say you are going to!

39 Display students' work nicely - and change it often.

40 Avoid giving an expectation of difficulty.

41 Think about the Chinese vase of self-esteem before losing your temper. See page 62.

42 Think about the Jackal and Giraffe before being sarcastic. See page 70.

43 Encourage 'brainstorming'.

44 Think about the room's arrangement and decoration.

45 Try to make standard activities more communicative.

46 Work towards a school culture of longer lessons.

    (90 minutes is better than 45 minutes. 3 hours is better still).

47 Have good quality teaching and learning time with your own children.

48 Use the 'shield' activity to get to know colleagues at a richer level.

49 Have a way of demonstrating brain/learning theory to students.

50 Join a group of teachers using a similar approach. See page 145.

51 Mentally check what's in your own 'Treasure Chest'. See page 19.

52 Have your personal collection of colour pens/scissors/blutak/drawing pins...

53 Do some deep breathing before each class.

54 Do some voice warm ups before each class.

55 Regularly give students something to learn by heart.

56 Keep a folder of 'ideas that work'.

57 Talk to colleagues about exciting developments in their subjects.

58 Look for cross-references between your subject and other subjects.

59 Try doing things (cleaning your teeth, for example) with your opposite hand.

60 Set objectives for yourself with different classes or students.

61 Each year/term make some teaching resolutions.

62 Don't do more than two hours' preparation or marking without a break.

63 Find ways to decorate and personalise your handouts.

64 Involve students in class management where possible.

65 Remember the 'Baboushka pen' when approaching lessons that bore you. See page 27.

66 Read through important information sometimes before you sleep.

67 Look at the Blobbies on page 77 before staff meetings.

68 Take time occasionally to run through an internal 'home movie' of a lesson and think about changes.

69 Develop a system for learning names quickly (and use the names often).

70 Get involved with a sport, amateur dramatics, music-making.

71 Have some 'positive thought' quotes around home and classroom.

72 Look at your class and identify intrapersonal intelligence.

73 Look at your class and identify a Kinaesthetic learner.

74 Regularly ask yourself 'What new thing am I learning here?'

75 Observe (generously) what students like about some other teachers.

76 Discuss acceptable/unacceptable student behaviour with colleagues.

77 Make your student 'reward' system more imaginative.

78 Check you are satisfied with your discipline system.

79 Be on time.

80 Raise your own and students' (and colleagues') expectations of success.

81 Encourage students to ask useful questions.

82 Tell students what you want them to do not what you don't want them to do.

And your own top tips.....

83

84

85

86

87

88

89

90

Ponder Point...

The good teacher in me remains in touch with the feeling of engagement in my own learning in order to make it available through my presence and evoke the same in my students. The ineffective teacher in me loses touch with the energy of engagement, leaving me tired and jaded, and my students bored and under-challenged, even by the same activity or material.
(Adrian Underhill, President, International Association of Teachers of English as a Foreign Language)

Assess your own position and mark the boxes a, b, c, or d.

a. I already do this   c. I might try this if I had some training

b. I'm prepared to try this   d. I would not try this in my teaching situation

Among the signs of a BRAIN-*friendly* approach to teaching you find:

Use of music		Use of dramatised texts	
Attractive pictures on walls		'Props box' for role play	
Appropiate energy level control		Very regular revision sessions	
Students using coloured highlighter pens		Students allowed to 'sleep' on new information	
Stretch breaks		Teacher awareness of different learning styles	
Use of visualisation		Games and role-plays to practise	
Supportive pair and group work		Encouragement and positive expectation	
Relaxation techniques		Students understanding rationale of method	
Concert readings		Fun and creativity	
Students aware of course syllabus		Signs that students are actively contributing	
Use of mind mapping		Lots of colour and interest	
Students' work is well displayed in class		Room arranged to allow easy movement	

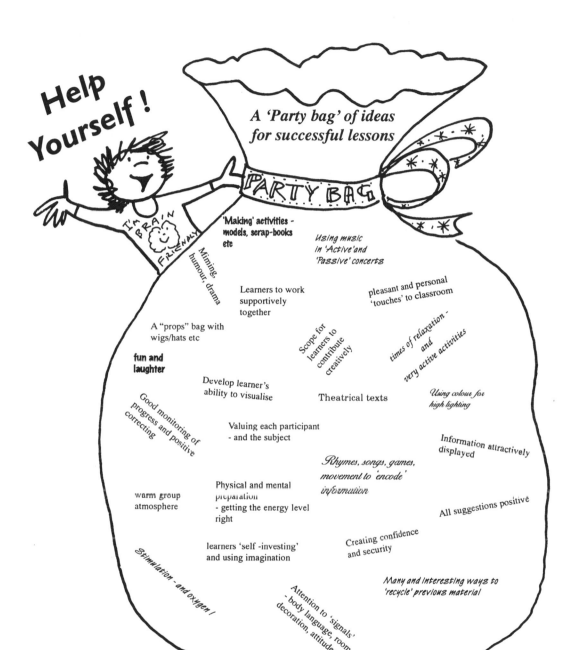

Help Yourself!

I'M BRAIN FRIENDLY

A 'Party bag' of ideas for successful lessons

PARTY BAG

'Making' activities - models, scrap-books etc

Using music in 'Active' and 'Passive' concerts

Miming, humour, drama

Learners to work supportively together

pleasant and personal 'touches' to classroom

A "props" bag with wigs/hats etc

Scope for learners to contribute creatively

times of relaxation - and very active activities

fun and laughter

Develop learner's ability to visualise

Theatrical texts

Using colour for high lighting

Good monitoring of progress and positive correcting

Valuing each participant - and the subject

Information attractively displayed

Rhymes, songs, games, movement to 'encode' information

warm group atmosphere

Physical and mental preparation - getting the energy level right

All suggestions positive

learners 'self -investing' and using imagination

Creating confidence and security

Stimulation - and oxygen!

Attention to 'signals' - body language, room decoration, attitudes

Many and interesting ways to 'recycle' previous material

Choose two coloured felt tip pens.
With one - highlight things that you do already.
With the other - highlight things you will work on.

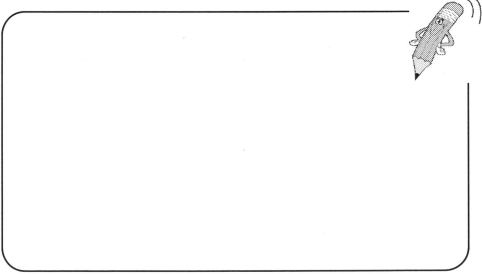

What needs to be pulled up and burned? See page 62.

Ponder Point... When I ask my father anythin' about lessons he always says he's forgotten 'cause it's so long since he was at school, and then he says I gotter work hard at school so's I'll know a lot when I'm grown up. Doesn't seem sense to me. Learnin' a lot of stuff jus' to forget it,... *(from William by Richmal Crompton)*

The basis of education is genuine respect for the human person. What then should education free us from?
From selfishness which leads to pride, closes men in, and causes unhappiness, tension, division, separation in families, groups, parties and even religions. *(Archbishop Helder Camara)* **Ponder Point...**

Ponder Point...

Education is not the filling of a pail, but the lighting of a fire. *(W.B.Yeats)*

The true teacher is the one who regards himself as a student of his students. *(Mahatma Gandhi)* **Ponder Point...**

Ponder Point...

Our challenge is to seize the once in a life-time opportunity to totally redesign learning to go with 'the grain of the brain'. *(John Abbott, President, 21st Century Learning Initiative)*

SOME SPECULATIONS . . .

At present, education is everywhere a topic of huge interest, and often considerable concern. World-wide, too many students 'truant inwardly'. Too many teachers feel over-stressed by ever increasing demands to 'deliver', or having to struggle constantly with demotivated students in poor learning environments. Such a situation has to change. What does the future hold?

• Education is about **enabling** - and that applies just as much to teachers as to students. (I am careful not to make a fossilizing distinction between teachers and learners!) Teacher training is likely to move further in the direction of recognising that teaching for success is not just the delivery of curriculum, but an on-going process of personal development for the individuals concerned. Valuing teachers for personal qualities, skills and experience, often gained outside the classroom and brought into it is relatively normal for students and parents - not always so for institutions and authorities. However, to be a teacher who is learning, and therefore changing, is generally not easy. It demands movement from the safe, the routine, the familiar into areas where the ceiling of expectation has been raised or even removed. Enabling this to happen needs proper concerned and effective support. Teaching is a serious business. There can, and should, be rigour as well as fun in Brain-friendly approaches. Certainly, we need to nurture the child inside each adult (not forgetting the adult in each child). Recognise the value of that child being 'alive and kicking' as it is the child that learns. That way we will dare to be different, and not give way to fear of failure.

• Rather than packing more and more into 'school' years we will move towards the creation of a 'learning society' (See jet plane page 31) in which life-long learning will be recognised as the norm.

• A minimum essential curriculum (global rather than national) will give all learners a good chance of knowing what we all must know whilst allowing faster learners time and scope to explore what they individually want to know.

• The challenge is to replace the Knowledge, Skills, Attitude (KSA) sequence of priorities in the traditional curriculum with an Attitude, Skills, Knowledge (ASK) sequence. This depends on much greater value being placed on 'positive attitudes' (responsibility, hopefulness, confidence and trust) and prioritising 'skills' (communication, team work, problem solving) above 'knowledge' which becomes increasingly easy for the informed learners to access on demand through the Internet. (I heard this vision well expressed by Sir Christopher Ball, Patron of the Campaign for Learning). Clearly everything we have thought about in the area of self-esteem, emotional intelligence, the 'Tango of Learning' is highly relevant to this.

- One personal speculation is that in twenty years' time it will be common for schools to have a music therapist (not called a music therapist) on the staff. This person will work on, literally, creating harmony in a learning environment, helping individuals to 'unblock', and facilitating access to more reflective mental processing of information.

- I am a member of the 'Learning and the Brain Forum' which brings together experts from the worlds of Science and Education to learn from each other, and in particular, to relate the latest scientific findings about the brain to questions of teaching and learning.

One thing which is very clear from this forum is that scientists are, rightly, very cautious about making sweeping claims about what they know. There is a real danger that, for example, a small scale piece of research is picked up by the popular press, over-simplified, and taken as a major authoritative statement. A lot of ill-informed 'Neuro-babble' is not helpful. However, the move towards a science-literate public is extremely helpful so that issues which affect ethics and policy are better understood. The frustration of writing this book is that it is unlikely to get the balance of science and classroom practice right for all readers, and that it can never be 'finished' because knowledge is moving forward all the time and at great pace. It is, however, offered as a serious contribution to encourage awareness and spark discussion amongst teachers. The vital debate, 'How do we learn?' 'How should we teach?' easily gets swamped in daily business. It needs to be kept constantly at the forefront of our relationship with the job.

- In the decades ahead our understanding of the complexities of the brain, the nature of memory and intelligence, and what exactly happens when learning occurs, will increase. As it does, we will re-found our education systems, our teaching, on a solid theory of learning.

The impact of this will be widespread, radical change. The BRAIN-friendly revolution, whose first stirrings we share in today, will have become a reality – and **we shall have helped to bring it about!**

A selection of Reading

I like short but interesting reading lists, and so have, quite arbitrarily, limited this to a very personal selection. As you see, some are straight off the best-seller list, whilst others may at first sight have no obvious connection with teaching... The books themselves, of course, have references to take the reader into greater detail.

✳ **The Human Brain-a guided tour** Susan Greenfield   Weidenfeld & Nicolson   ISBN 0 29781 69 2
Susan Greenfield is Professor of Pharmacology at Oxford University and Director of the Royal Institution
I have relied heavily on this book for up to date information on the brain.

✳ **The Everyday Genius** Peter Kline   Great Ocean Publishers, Inc USA   ISBN 0 915556 18 9
Very practical observations and ideas for joyful learning.

✳ **The Man who mistook his Wife for a Hat**   Oliver Sachs   Picador   ISBN 0 33029491 1
Classic enthralling case-study guide to the extraordinariness of the human mind.

✳ **Mapping the Mind**   Rita Carter   Weidenfeld & Nicolson
Beautifully designed, well referenced, and accessible overview of brain topics.

✳ **Music and the Mind**   Paul Robertson   Contact made through website www.esws.co.uk.robertson
Excellent study of this key subject- with CDs available.

✳ **Unicorns are Real**   Barbara Meister-Vitale   Warner Books Inc , 666 Fifth Ave, New York USA
Useful little paperback, particularly for working with 'Right hemisphere' learners.

✳ **Brain Gym**   Paul and Gail Denison   Edu-Kinesthetics, Inc PO 3396 Ventura, CA 93006-3396 USA
This is the slim, original, family friendly introduction to the activites.

✳ **How the Mind Works**   Stephen Pinker   Penguin Press   ISBN 0-713-991305
A solid, information-packed study. Very readable for those pursuing the subject.

✳ **The Road to Daybreak**   Henri Nouwen   Darton Longman Todd   ISBN 0 232 51849 1
A thoughtful meditative study of deep issues by the Dutch theologian.

✳ **Community and Growth**   Jean Vanier   Darton Longman Todd   ISBN 0 232 51 450 X
Profound, sensitive, joyful and painful account of relationships by the founder of the L'Arche communities.

✳ **Emotional Intelligence**   Daniel Goleman   Bloomsbury   ISBN 0 7475 2622 2
In case you haven't read it already.

✳ **Use your head**   Tony Buzan   BBC Books   ISBN 0 56320812 0
One of his many popular books on Mindmapping and learning strategies.

✳ **Frames of Mind**   Howard Gardner   Paladin   ISBN 0-586-08506-8
An influential book in launching the important Multiple Intelligences debate.

✳ **Memory Meaning & Method**   Earl W Stevick   Newbury House Inc. ISBN 0-88377-053-9
For many years a valuable overview read, especially for language teachers.

✳ **The Learning Adventure**   Eva Hoffman   ISBN 095 35 38 702
Affective skills activities for children and young people presented appropriately for their age group

✳ **In Your Hands**   Jane Revell and Susan Norman   Saffire Press   ISBN 1 90156400 2
NLP for language teaching in particular, but also a very accessible and congruent general introduction.

✳ **The Way of a Child**   A C Harwood   Rudolph Steiner Press   ISBN 0 85440 182 2   First published in 1940
Interesting ideas to re-visit and ponder.

✳ **Anatomy of Choice in Education**   Roland Meighan & Philip Toogood   Education Now Books
ISBN 1-871526-07-8   Some structurally challenging concepts.

✳ **Opening Minds** Valerie Bayliss Royal Society of Arts 8 John Adam St London WC2N 6EZ   ISBN 0-901-469386

✳ **Hare brain, Tortoise mind** Guy Claxton   Fourth Estate   ISBN 1-85702-451-6
Interesting exploration of intuition, unconscious perception and how to value it.

✳ **Accelerated Learning in practice**   Alister Smith   Network Educational Press   ISBN 1-85539-048-5
Well referenced and systematic - relating to school situations

✳ **Principled Headship: a Teacher's Guide to the Galaxy**   Terry O'Mahony   Crown House Publishing
ISBN 1-899836-403

..and, although this is a 'reading' list, let's not forget films on 'Teaching for Success', such as **Dead Poets' Society**, and **Jonathan Livingstone Seagull.**

Challenge

What two book titles would **you** add?
And what film / play has given you an important insight into teaching?

Contact some of these organisations

CAMPAIGN FOR LEARNING

19 Buckingham Street London WC2N 6EE
Tel: 020 7930 1111 Fax: 020 7930 1551
Email: tgreany@cflearning.org.uk
An imaginative and widely supported UK initiative to promote life long learning – in schools, businesses, and families in the community.

ENGLISH EXPERIENCE

25 Julian Road, Folkestone, Kent CT19 5HW, England
Telephone/Fax: (44) 1303 226702
Email: englishexperience@dial.pipex.com
http://www.brain-friendly.com
English Experience publish educational materials and offer training in brain-friendly methodology. Brain-friendly is a registered trade mark of English Experience.™

SEAL (Society for Effective Affective Learning)

POBox 2246, Bath BA1 2YR
Tel: 01225 466244 Fax: 01225 444024
http://www.seal.org.uk
SEAL is an international educational charity with members in over forty countries. SEAL operates in three main areas: Education; Management training; and Personal development. Its objectives are to empower individuals to discover their own learning potential, and to transform attitudes in educational institutions.
*To do this, it organises major conferences, provides a data base, offers networking opportunities, and arranges training in the methodologies discussed in **Teaching for Success**.*

The Royal Society of Arts

8 John Adam St. London WC2N 6EZ
Tel: 020 7930 5115
Leslie James, Head of Education
Important forum for the discussion of educational issues.
*Recently published the **Opening Minds** report.*

UNESCO

Education International
5, Boulevard du Roi Albert 11
B-1210 Brussels
http://www.education.unesco.org
Provides a worldwide vision for improving opportunities

Index

Acknowledgements

There are many people who, by their writing or involvement in thinking about the brain and how we learn, have stimulated my interest and encouraged me to write this book. I would like to mention four in particular.

Peter O'Connell, for whom I worked for many years and who, amongst other contributions, founded the Society for Effective Affective Learning, and introduced Suggestopedia to Western Europe.

Michael Lawlor, Co-founder and long term President of SEAL whose example of lifelong learning was inspirational to all who knew him.

Sir Christopher Ball, Patron of the Campaign for Learning, Chancellor of Derby University and my tutor many years ago, whose thinking on education continues to be radical and influential at the highest level.

And finally, my youngest son John, whose personal struggles and triumphs in learning have challenged and delighted our family and demonstrated that it well becomes each of us to raise our own levels of expectation.

About the Author

Mark Fletcher M.A. (Oxon.), P.G.Cert.Ed.T.E.F.L., Dip.T.E.F.L.A.

Since qualifying as a teacher in 1972, Mark has had experience of Secondary school and Technical College teaching; running a language school; working with under 11's; In-company 'skills' training; Adult education and, particularly in recent years, of travelling widely all over the world helping groups of teachers develop BRAIN-*friendly* classroom methodology.

He is a BBC World Service speaker, educational advisor for the year 2000 "Whole Learner" series, and a Trustee of SEAL (Society for Effective Affective Learning). He is also the Academic Director of **English Experience**, a school set up to pioneer BRAIN-*friendly* teaching, and author of many popular teaching materials.

Mark's world wide seminar tours, keynote Conference lectures, and popular teaching materials have encouraged thousands of teachers to develop their own brain-friendly skills.

He is a member of the 'Learning and the Brain' Forum organised by the Lifelong Learning Foundation to explore the inter-face between Education and Neuro-science.